HOW TO WIN YOUR CASE IN TRAFFIC COURT WITHOUT A LAWYER

By Janet Traken

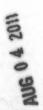

HOW TO WIN YOUR CASE IN TRAFFIC COURT WITHOUT A LAWYER

Copyright © 2011 Atlantic Publishing Group, Inc.
1405 SW 6th Avenue • Ocala, Florida 34471 • Phone 800-814-1132 • Fax 352-622-1875
Web site: www.atlantic-pub.com • E-mail: sales@atlantic-pub.com
SAN Number: 268-1250

Library of Congress Cataloging-in-Publication Data

Traken, Janet, 1955-
  How to win your case in traffic court without a lawyer / by Janet Traken.
      p. cm.
  Includes bibliographical references and index.
  ISBN-13: 978-1-60138-305-1 (alk. paper)
  ISBN-10: 1-60138-305-3 (alk. paper)
  1. Traffic courts--United States--Popuar works. 2. Traffic violations--United States--Popuar works. I. Title.
  KF2232.T73 2010
  345.73'0247--dc22
                        2009048431

PROJECT MANAGER: Kimberly Fulscher • EDITORIAL INTERN: Amber McDonald
INTERIOR DESIGN: Antoinette D'Amore • addesign@videotron.ca
COVER DESIGN: Jackie Miller • millerjackiej@gmail.com

Printed on Recycled Paper

Printed in the United States

We recently lost our beloved pet "Bear," who was not only our best and dearest friend but also the "Vice President of Sunshine" here at Atlantic Publishing. He did not receive a salary but worked tirelessly 24 hours a day to please his parents. Bear was a rescue dog that turned around and showered myself, my wife, Sherri, his grandparents Jean, Bob, and Nancy, and every person and animal he met (maybe not rabbits) with friendship and love. He made a lot of people smile every day.

We wanted you to know that a portion of the profits of this book will be donated to The Humane Society of the United States. *—Douglas & Sherri Brown*

The human-animal bond is as old as human history. We cherish our animal companions for their unconditional affection and acceptance. We feel a thrill when we glimpse wild creatures in their natural habitat or in our own backyard.

Unfortunately, the human-animal bond has at times been weakened. Humans have exploited some animal species to the point of extinction.

The Humane Society of the United States makes a difference in the lives of animals here at home and worldwide. The HSUS is dedicated to creating a world where our relationship with animals is guided by compassion. We seek a truly humane society in which animals are respected for their intrinsic value, and where the human-animal bond is strong.

Want to help animals? We have plenty of suggestions. Adopt a pet from a local shelter, join The Humane Society and be a part of our work to help companion animals and wildlife. You will be funding our educational, legislative, investigative and outreach projects in the U.S. and across the globe.

Or perhaps you'd like to make a memorial donation in honor of a pet, friend or relative? You can through our Kindred Spirits program. And if you'd like to contribute in a more structured way, our Planned Giving Office has suggestions about estate planning, annuities, and even gifts of stock that avoid capital gains taxes.

Maybe you have land that you would like to preserve as a lasting habitat for wildlife. Our Wildlife Land Trust can help you. Perhaps the land you want to share is a backyard— that's enough. Our Urban Wildlife Sanctuary Program will show you how to create a habitat for your wild neighbors.

So you see, it's easy to help animals. And The HSUS is here to help.

THE HUMANE SOCIETY
OF THE UNITED STATES.

2100 L Street NW • Washington, DC 20037 • 202-452-1100
www.hsus.org

TRADEMARK DISCLAIMER

TABLE OF CONTENTS

CHAPTER 10: PREPARING FOR THE TRIAL STEP TWO: ORGANIZING YOUR CASE.......................... 153

FOREWORD

Traffic tickets represent a multi-million dollar source of revenue for local and state governments in the United States. Police forces have officers whose entire job is to ticket drivers for violating traffic laws. In fact, this industry has become so profitable private companies are now in the mix, issuing tickets via privately owned traffic cameras to drivers running red lights. The success of this entire industry, however, relies on one key assumption: The driver will not fight the ticket.

Because of the way our court system is set up, it is not surprising that many drivers choose not to fight their tickets. To many drivers, courts are institutions veiled in mystery. From complicated procedures to vague laws, the system seems set up to keep all but those with specialized training from willingly entering the courthouse. This is unfortunate. The court system should be a place where everyday individuals find a forum to protect them from the excesses of government. *How to Win Your Case In Traffic Court Without a Lawyer* provides an invaluable service by helping to open the doors of our courthouses to every person.

Fighting a traffic ticket is not as difficult as most think. The first step in any dealings with the legal system is to know the law. It used to be that knowing and understanding the law was nearly impossible for someone without formal legal training. Up until about decade ago, the only way to find the law was to learn to navigate several legal resources. A good portion of law school was devoted to teaching future lawyers just these skills. With the rise of Web resources, however, this is no longer the case. Now, knowing and understanding the law is little more than an Internet search away. Each state has made its statutes available online.

Increasingly, state courts are doing the same for their cases. Sites like Findlaw (**www.findlaw.com**) and Justia (**www.justia.com**) provide more legal resources. And myriad blogs publish timely, expert legal analysis on every area of the law. *How to Win Your Case In Traffic Court Without a Lawyer* provides even more resources to aid drivers in fighting their tickets.

The next step in fighting a ticket is to figure out how your particular facts apply to that law. As *How to Win Your Case In Traffic Court Without a Lawyer* astutely points out, this involves a careful reading of the statute under which you are charged and figuring out how the facts of your case work within the framework of that law. The biggest mistake I see those who represent themselves make is failing to argue how the particular facts in their case prove their innocence under the law. Many "pro se" (without a lawyer) defendants come into court and set out sympathetic stories on why you should feel sorry for them. Unfortunately, those stories rarely are relevant to the law the court is applying. Judges are constrained by the law they administer. And a driver who is unable to tailor her argument to the relevant law is unlikely to prevail at trial.

Applying facts to law is a hard skill to master. It involves long hours of research, trying to find cases where a court ruled in the defendant's favor based on facts that are similar to yours.

A big value of *How to Win Your Case In Traffic Court Without a Lawyer* is the research is already done for you. Janet Traken has taken the time to go through each major traffic offense and set out the facts that would prove your innocence at trial. All that is left to the reader is to find the offense, find the matching facts, and employ the arguments laid out. Janet Traken could not have made it more simple.

The final step to fighting a ticket is to appear in court. This is probably the most daunting part for pro se defendants. The key to prevailing in court is, very simply, to know your rights. One thing that people who are not in court every day don't realize is just like everyone you know, there are judges of every type: good and bad; smart and lazy; compassionate and bullish. While everyone hopes to draw a thoughtful, intelligent, and compassionate judge, this doesn't always happen. Many judges are impatient, especially when it comes to pro se parties. The defendant who knows his rights, however, can get past this.

When dealing with a judge, it is important to be willing to speak. While, to be sure, defendants should treat the court and the judge with respect, this does not mean sitting by idly. The best pro se parties are the ones who take a firm, but respectful tone with the court and, accordingly, demand the rights afforded to them. To be able to do this effectively, however, you must first know your rights.

The most impressive aspect of *How to Win Your Case In Traffic Court Without a Lawyer* is how it both gives drivers the tools to demand these rights and encourages them to do so. Throughout the book, Janet Traken explains to the reader their rights in the court and how to exercise them. There are many cases I have sat through where the pro se party should have ultimately prevailed. Judges are neutral parties in any dispute; therefore, they cannot assert rights for you and cannot help one party to the detriment of another. Consequently, when a pro se party does not know his or her rights (or is afraid to assert them), he or she can ultimately lose an otherwise winnable case. Before you go into court, know your rights. Also, follow the advice of this book and don't be afraid to assert yourself.

The entire traffic ticket system is founded on the assumption individuals will not fight their tickets. Many drivers pay fines on tickets based on questionable facts. If you think this applies to your situation, don't let the apprehension of appearing in court deter you from asserting your rights. Read this book. Learn the law. Understand your rights. Undermine the assumption. Fight your ticket.

Garrett S. Ledgerwood
Editor in Chief, *Washington and Lee Law Review*, Volume 66

INTRODUCTION

Have a conversation with any police officer and ask her why she hands out speeding tickets. All police officers will tell you the same thing, "To help reduce accidents and keep the roads safe." But in an article by Belinda Rachman, Esq. titled "What Does a Traffic Ticket Really Cost You," Rachman said, "The cost of paying and training a traffic officer is approximately $75,000 per year, but he or she can issue between $150,000 to $200,000 in citations. How many businesses can claim that rate of return?"

Rachman goes on to say that in towns like New Rome, Ohio, and Waldo, Florida, "over 70 percent of their operating budget comes from the fines generated by moving violations." While the speeding ticket is the most commonly used tool to deter drivers from speeding, studies show these tickets do little to keep people from repeatedly speeding.

A study published in *Traffic Injury Prevention* in March 2007, titled "Do Speeding Tickets Reduce the Likelihood of Receiving Subsequent Speeding Tickets? A Longitudinal Study of Speeding Violators in Maryland," identified 3,739,951 Maryland drivers who were followed for one year. The study was conducted by Saranath Lawpoolsri and Jingyi Li of the Department of Epidemiology and Preventive Medicine, University of Maryland School of Medicine, and Elisa R. Braver of the National Study Center for Trauma and Emergency Medical Service in Baltimore, Maryland.

According to their findings, receiving a speeding ticket made drivers twice as likely to receive a consequent ticket within the next year compared to drivers who were not ticketed that month. This means drivers caught speeding were not bothered by the legal ramifications of the tickets and continued to speed.

This study notes speeding ticket recipients drive at least ten miles over the speed limit on a consistent basis, so the ticket is an ineffective means of curbing the lead-footed behavior.

Lawpoolsri, Li, and Braver state an officer's decision to ticket a driver, rather than to warn the driver not to speed again, could be based on the driver's prior driving record, but the officers do not normally check the driving record of the driver. Therefore, the decision to ticket is based more on the officer's involvement in a traffic enforcement unit, how the officer evaluates the driver's attitude when caught, and by how much the driver was speeding.

How to Win Your Case in Traffic Court Without a Lawyer was written in light of the growing number of people who get traffic tickets every year; many of which are unwarranted. Remember, the success of law enforcement depends on its ability to create a meaningful deterrent threat to road users. And with the rising cost of attorney's fees, many drivers think it is just easier to pay the ticket and move on. After all, why spend all that money on a pricey attorney when you can just pay a fine of a few hundred dollars and move on?

Drivers who think this way are incorrect — on many occasions, you can fight your ticket and win, without the financial burden of a high-priced attorney. When you choose to argue against the ticket, you have nothing to lose and everything to gain. Some of the benefits include:

- Avoiding potentially increased car insurance rates

- Avoiding additional points on your driver's license

- Feeling good about standing up for yourself

- Avoiding the possible professional consequences that traffic tickets can bring, especially if you hold a commercial driver's license or a professional license such as a doctor or attorney

Each day, an estimated 100,000 drivers receive a traffic ticket. While many municipalities try to keep the actual numbers confidential, it quickly adds up. Traffic enforcement officials write a combined 25 million to 50 million tickets each year — and that number does not include parking tickets. In many cases, the officer writing the ticket knows if you even attempt to fight it, you will win.

The U.S. government is committed to motorist safety. Most police officers who write traffic tickets do so in hopes that drivers will, in fact, alter their driving patterns. The National Highway Traffic Safety Administration has a government-maintained Web site that includes studies on traffic safety; updates to traffic law; articles on policies, laws, safety, annual assessments, and organization charts; ways to inspect your vehicle; information on recalls; and ways to report safety violations. Visit the site at **www.nhtsa.dot.gov**.

Other than safety reasons, many officers write tickets because the revenue goes to the city. Revenues are a large source of income for many municipalities. According to Troy Simpson, President and CEO of TraffiCare International, LLC, "Traffic tickets are a multi-billion dollar industry, ranking just behind Sony, BMW, McDonald's, and several others." Do the math: If you assume the average fine from a traffic ticket is roughly $150, the profit for municipalities is somewhere between $3.75 billion to $7.5 billion dollars. There is no other class of "crime" that brings as much profit to state and local governments, but it does not stop there. Figure in the additional revenue for insurance companies, and there is even more money added to the equation. The average increase in insurance rates for a speeding ticket is $300 over a period of three years, adding another several billion dollars to the equation.

Another reason officers write so many tickets is because, in many cases, their performance is at least partially based on how many tickets they write. In many small towns, not much crime happens, but there is a straight stretch of highway that runs through the outskirts. You will often see cruisers sitting in the medians, waiting for the opportunity to pull someone over. Not only does this activity bring in additional revenue for their small town, but it also provides them with a little boost on their performance records.

Individuals normally do not protest incidents like these because they do not like to make waves with the law and as a result, rarely fight the traffic tickets they are issued. Statistics indicate that about 5 percent of motorists who are issued a ticket fight it. In Vermont, for example, in 2008 and 2009, 111,322 tickets were issued, only 19,207 of which were contested. Of those, 10,295 were dismissed prior to hearing.

You are a well-informed motorist — one who will not take a traffic ticket lying down. When you purchased this book, you took the first step in fighting that ticket. Although ticket quotas are illegal in the United States, officers everywhere will write many tickets every day. In addition to that, many officers show up in court on their days off, which means they are paid overtime to be there. That is one of the reasons they may write you a citation for driving 65 mph in a 60 mph zone, even if you were driving safely.

Navigating the legal system can be a tricky and intimidating thing. The maze of forms to fill out, dates to keep straight, and official-looking clerks who man the counters and courtrooms may discourage you. However, it is entirely in your benefit to take the legal leap. Court costs, attorney fees, and increased insurance premiums from just one ticket can cost hundreds of extra dollars a year. Armed with this book and some additional materials, you can successfully piece together a defense that will prepare you for trial.

Remember, if this is your first ticket, you are in an excellent position. The easiest ticket to fight is your first. Even if you are unquestionably guilty, the chance of getting a satisfying plea offer is best when you have a clean record. The catch is you need to fight to get the plea offer.

Even if you fully intend to take responsibility for the violation, it makes sense to proceed with fighting the ticket. This will give you the opportunity to speak with the prosecutor about the possibility of a deal before you plead guilty.

How to Win Your Case in Traffic Court Without a Lawyer is divided in sections so you can easily understand the information. Since laws and preparing for a trial can be so confusing, this book was written for the average driver who does not spend his or her day leafing through law books.

While this book does cover moving violations extensively, nonmoving violations are covered only briefly. These tickets truly have no adverse consequences on your license and insurance rates, so while they are worth mentioning, they are not essential to the overall objective of this book. The overall objective is to prepare you to fight a traffic ticket. This book will walk you through the following:

- The first steps to take when you get a ticket

- How to research and understand the law under which you were cited

- The types of moving violations and what they truly mean

- The negative effects of a traffic ticket

- What traffic school can and cannot do for you and your case

- Deciding whether to fight the ticket or pay

- Special considerations for truck drivers and others who need a clean license as a condition of their employment

- Determining if you need a lawyer

- Preparing for trial

- A discussion about alcohol-related offenses

Within these pages, you will find Chapter 8 devoted to gathering and analyzing your evidence. You can expect to learn how to collect your own evidence and effectively prepare for a trial. I will discuss organizing your case by preparing your testimony in advance, and also prepping your witness and your questions for him or her, and the officer. Learn what to expect the first time you enter the courtroom, how to settle your case without the trial itself, and how to handle yourself should the case go all the way to trial. While I cannot promise you will win your trial, I can promise that after reading this book, you will be able to give it an impressive shot. Throughout the book you will find case studies from a professional truck driver, an insurance agent, and other everyday people who have had to deal with traffic tickets.

There are certain limitations to this book. While I devote a chapter to alcohol-related offenses, do not try to fight one of these without the assistance of a lawyer. If you have received a traffic ticket for an offense that could put you in jail, you should seek the assistance of a professional in this area of the law. The same holds true for any traffic ticket that is a result of a car accident in which the other party was injured in any way. The stakes are much higher when someone else has been injured, and you cannot navigate this type of case alone.

With that said, grab your highlighter and a pen. There is a lot of information in these pages and you will likely be taking some notes. The strategies in this book could work for you and can save you money.

CHAPTER 1

You Have Received a Traffic Ticket: Now What?

It is 5:30 on a Friday afternoon and you are fighting traffic on the freeway. The sun is shining and your day could not end fast enough — all you want to do is get home. With your mind wandering through the events of the day, you cruise along, keeping steady with the flow of traffic.

You are surprised when you see the flashing red and blue lights in the rearview mirror. You put on your turn signal and merge to the right lane, getting out of the way, certain the police car will fly right by you, but it does not. You realize the police car is pulling you over. As you signal again and merge to the breakdown lane, your heart catches in your throat and your breath quickens. That sinking feeling of panic sets in and you know you are about to get a ticket.

After signing on the dotted line of your traffic ticket, you are likely outraged, shocked, or angry. You were going with the flow of traffic, right? Why did the officer stop you and not that kid in the red convertible who went flying by you? When you tried to ask the question, the officer was evasive and said he clocked you going 15 mph over the posted speed limit. In the back of your mind, you know you were not going that fast, or were you? You know for sure you were not driving unsafely. Inevitably, doubt starts to creep in and as you think about it you sigh, tossing the ticket on the front passenger seat, resigned you will have to pay it. After all, it is the police. They are relying on you not fighting.

Jotting Down Notes of the Incident

You are not the first person to ever get a traffic ticket, so rest assured you are not alone. You are not even the first person the officer has issued a ticket to on his shift. Take a moment to calm down, collect your thoughts, and jot some notes. If you have purchased this book because you received a citation a few weeks ago, it is not too late to do this exercise. The sooner you can jot some notes down on paper, the better.

Be specific in your notes — jot down:

- Exactly where you were

- The conditions of the road and traffic

- The weather conditions

- Whether you were in the passing or driving lane

- Whether the officer told you where he clocked you

- Whether the officer was sitting in his car or was standing on the side of the road

- Approximately how far from where he was to where you were pulled over

If you are still sitting on the side of the road, this note-taking serves two purposes. It will keep the details fresh for future reference, and it gives the officer time to finish his or her notes, pull out from behind you, and drive away. If you have a camera with you (or a cell phone with a photo-taking feature), get out of the car and take some pictures while you are still sitting in the exact location where you were pulled over. If it has been a few weeks, go back and take the pictures now and also try to do it at the same time of day you were pulled over.

Photos are incredibly helpful during this process and particularly during the trial phase. Any photos you take should be enlarged for a trial. At a minimum, make them 8- by 10-inch photos, but 11- by 17-inch photos would be ideal. You do not have to be the person who took the photos; however, you will need to confirm the photos are an accurate depiction of the scene of the crime at the time the crime was committed.

Look for and capture:

- Obscured traffic signals and signs.

- Actual road obstructions that would reduce visibility, such as construction equipment in the median or snow banks during the winter.

- How the road looks from your driver's seat, at the place you were pulled over.

- Show that the road was straight if it indeed was. You can use this to help prove that your speed was safe, even if it was above the posted speed limit.

- The traffic and how heavy it is during the time of day you were pulled over.

- Speed limit signs and other road signs.

- A photo from the position of the police car. Could anything have blocked his or her sight?

Also, using your odometer, time how far it is to where he or she pulled you over. At first, this may seem like a senseless exercise, but it is not. It will serve you well later on in this process.

Finally, diagram the road or intersection where you were pulled over. Be sure to capture any specifics such as direction of traffic, positions of both yours and the officer's cars, and any one-way roads or traffic signals. This is also a good place to note if there were any obstructions in the way of your viewing of the speed limit signs.

Reading and Understanding Your Ticket

Now, take a look at the ticket. Make sure you find the date for your arraignment and write it on a calendar — the date is pertinent. If you think you are going to forget it, put it on a note and tape it to your door, so you see it every day when you walk out.

If you forget your arraignment date and fail to appear in court, you run the risk of having a bench warrant issued for your arrest. A simple moving violation can quickly snowball to a misdemeanor charge in many states. Other states will automatically suspend your license without any warning. Do not let this happen to you.

Next, call the court clerk's office and ask what you need to do to plead "not guilty," and get a court date. You can find this number in the phone book or on the Web site for the court in which you are to appear. Regardless of the facts that surround your traffic stop, always ask for this court date. Not only will this give you time to emotionally prepare and grasp the full scope of what is going on, it will give you time to investigate the laws that were cited and to determine if you actually did violate a statute. The law makes it truly easy for you to plead guilty and pay a fine. Under U.S. law, you are innocent until proven guilty. However, the officer will provide his side of the story.

Next, look at all the boxes on your ticket. Be sure the information is right. Double-check the date and time as it was written. Is the description of your vehicle, driver's license number, and license plate number correct? While courts will often excuse minor errors on a ticket, they will not excuse major errors such as a gross misidentification of your vehicle or citing the wrong location on the ticket. If some of the most basic details are incorrect, your ticket could be deemed invalid and your case could be dismissed.

Finally, stop at your local office supply store and buy a three-ring binder to keep all your notes, pictures, and papers. This ensures you will not lose anything, as you will have all the important papers you need at your fingertips.

CASE STUDY: TRAFFIC
TICKETS: INJUSTICE OR
INVALUABLE?

Traffic stops are the only way most Americans ever interact with the police during the year. In fact, more than half of the police's "contact" with civilians is due to routine traffic stops. While most of us get annoyed at the thought of being pulled over to receive a warning or a ticket, some studies prove that citations might actually benefit society in a number of ways.

The first benefit might seem obvious: many larger crimes are detected as a result of traffic violations. It seems rational that men and women who commit crimes off-road tend to do so on the road as well. When New York serial killer Joel Rifkin sped away from cops trying to cite him for a missing license plate, they pursued and found a murdered prostitute in his truck. Ted Bundy, David Berkowitz (Son of Sam), and Timothy McVeigh were all caught because of minor traffic violations. While in Florida, Mohammed Atta and two other 9/11 terrorists accumulated several speeding tickets; Atta even had a warrant out for his arrest for skipping a traffic court appearance.

Of course, these are extreme examples, but every year police uncover stashes of weapons, drugs, and drivers with outstanding warrants during routine stops. In fact, most crimes committed in the United States each year involve driving. This is partially because our country is so expansive that owning a vehicle is almost required to get around, and partially because most citizens do not consider traffic violations to be "real" crimes. Consider this: In 2008, former Giants receiver Plaxico Burress pled guilty to accidently shooting himself in the thigh with an unregistered gun and was sentenced to two years in prison. However, for accidentally killing a man while driving drunk, NFL receiver Donté Stallworth was sentenced to one month of county jail and two years of house arrest in June 2009.

The second benefit of traffic tickets is they help reduce deaths. In fact, there is often a direct correlation between the number of citations officers make and the amount of fatal accidents in an area. In a recent Transportation Alternatives study based in New York City (and mirrored elsewhere), it was found that, from 2001 to 2006, the number of fatalities caused by speeding rose 11 percent — while, at the same time, the summons issued for speeding dropped 22 percent. Between 2005 and 2007, there was a 12 percent drop in summons for not yielding, and the number of deaths caused as a result of the same traffic violation rose 26 percent.

Another commonly held belief is too much attention is given to minor traffic infractions in major cities where there are far worse problems, such as violent crime and drugs. But recent studies by the Department of Justice's new program, Data-Driven Approaches to Crime and Traffic Safety (DDACTS), show that there is a link between geographic location, crime, and car accidents. DDACTS places "highly visible" officers in major cities like Baltimore, in areas with high concentrations of traffic violations and other criminal activity. As a result, these cities are seeing less of both problems. Thus, the third benefit of traffic tickets is demonstrated: increased public safety.

George Kelling, a former probation officer, originated the "broken windows" theory in the 1980s, which observed that a building with broken windows invites even more vandalism — since they make it seem like no one cares. Major cities often have this same problem in "hot spots" where people run red lights, disregard blinkers, and drive recklessly. The DDACTS reflects the "broken windows" theory with what it is trying to accomplish: showing that someone cares.

CHAPTER 2

Determining What You Are Charged With

The most important initial consideration when deciding whether to fight a traffic ticket is to know what you are being charged with. A traffic ticket will indicate, usually through a code number, what offense you as the driver have committed. There are statues and ordinances in each state, which are published and correspond to every traffic violation. Cornell University Law School maintains an excellent Web site that contains the statutes for every state: **www.law.cornell.edu/statutes.html**. Local ordinances are generally published on the locality's Web site or are available upon request. The key skill you need to build an excellent defense is the ability to understand and research these statutes or ordinances under which you have been charged.

This chapter will cover where to start your legal research, items to look for while you are researching, the two types of traffic violations, and the three types of speeding violations.

Where to Start Your Legal Research

To prepare an appropriate defense, you need to fully understand the law you have been charged with. On your ticket, there will be a citation code and a brief description of the statute that you have been charged with violating. This description will be vague and most likely say something such as, "speeding 5 to 10 mph above posted limit." While this vague description may be correct, look up this specific citation code to find out precisely what the wording says.

Using a search engine is normally the quickest and most efficient way to research your state's statutes. Type in the traffic statute and the name of your state in quotations. For example, "Title 29-A §1251 Maine." Inserting the quotations tells the search engine you are searching for all the words together, exactly as you have typed them. This way, you do not run the risk of wading through traffic statutes for a dozen other states before you find your own, or worse yet, getting a million unrelated results that you have to skim through.

If you are not comfortable using the Internet or you do not have access, go to your local library. Take your ticket with you and ask to see the reference librarian. He or she can help point you in the right direction. A word of caution when it comes to using the library to do legal research: Books are not frequently updated. Updated information is printed on a leaflet and placed in either the front or back cover of the book.

When you find the statute you are charged under, print it out or make a copy and carefully look it over. Analyze the wording and phrasing of the law. When reading the statute you are charged with, you will likely find it complex, confusing, and so wordy it almost does not make sense. However, this is in your favor.

Although this seems tedious, it is an important exercise. Write down each section of the law and all of its subsections as separate line items on a piece of paper. After you have done that, read any other sections that are referenced in the original section you allegedly violated. You will find that by the time you are done writing down all of these individual sections, you will have quite a list, but you want it this way. It affords you more opportunity to argue the validity of your ticket.

Now, go through each line item and determine whether what is written truly applies to your citation. For each section that does apply, cross it off. For each section that is questionable, leave it alone, as you will come back to it.

This exercise will help because your officer could have cited the wrong law. Frequently, if you study the statute carefully, you will find that technically what you did is not a violation of the exact words of the statute. This way, it is easier to effectively determine if you violated every element of the statute you are charged with. The state must prove you violated every element of the statute you are charged under. If the state cannot prove every element, you are not guilty.

This could be an innocent mistake and the officer just misinterpreted the statute he or she cited you under, or the officer could have written down the wrong one. Other times, the officer may have known exactly what he or she was doing and purposely tried to squeeze your infraction into a statute that did not fit the crime.

Another important note when reviewing the statutes: Be sure to review not only the section you are charged with, but also all of the subsections before and after it. While the section you have been charged under may indicate that you are guilty, another subsection may offer a substantial defense in your favor.

For example, say you were charged with speeding. The officer cited a statute on your ticket that indicates your speed was based on a reading from a radar gun. When you research this statute, you find a subsection that states an officer must follow certain procedures when using a radar gun. If you can prove that he did not follow those specific procedures, you can prove your innocence.

Remember, when using the Internet to look up your traffic infraction, always be sure you are reading the most up-to-date version of the law. The wording can be revised frequently and new sections are added all the time, so you have to be on the lookout for updated information.

CASE STUDY: BE PREPARED BEFORE TRAFFIC COURT

Nicole Orr
Writer and Editor
Ocala, Florida

I remember it like it was yesterday.

I was on my way to traffic school to get the points off my license from a speeding ticket I had received a few months earlier. My friend was in the car with me, as he was also attending traffic school for a ticket.

Suddenly, there were lights flashing behind me; I was being pulled over. The cop informed me I had gone straight in a turn-only lane that was a turn-only lane during certain hours of the day. The problem, aside from the fact that I had just been pulled over and given a ticket on my way to traffic school, was that I actually was not in that lane when I went through the intersection. With my friend in the car telling me I was not daydreaming about what actually happened, I decided to challenge the ticket in traffic court. I figured it was the best option for dealing with the ticket, especially because it is common thinking that police officers never show up for traffic court — that they have better things to do with their time.

Whoever put that idea out there was wrong. The day of my traffic hearing, I was filled with anxiety. I had never stood in front of a judge before, and I was so worked up. Nothing could calm my nerves, not even the thought that the officer probably wouldn't show.

As I sat on the hard, wooden benches waiting for the judge to call my case, I scanned the area where the police officers were sitting. There were quite a few present, a surprising amount in fact, and I didn't recognize anyone as being familiar. I figured I was safe. It wasn't until I was called to the podium to give my statement that I realized my officer was there.

I had an argument and a defense ready, but I wasn't prepared enough. It went out the window as soon as I stood to give my defense. The experience, overall, was mortifying and nerve-racking. I still had to pay the fine, and I still got points on my license. And, on top of it, I missed a day of class just to try and remove the ticket from my record and save a couple hundred bucks. People brush traffic court off all the time like it's a giveaway to get out of a ticket. Let me tell you, it's not. Arrive at traffic court fully prepared: know the exact statute you received a ticket for, research and know every detail about it, understand how you will be able to argue your case, and always remain calm. Police officers sometimes do attend traffic court trials, so be prepared to effectively challenge your ticket with a valid defense.

Two Types of Traffic Violations

There are two types of traffic violations: moving and non-moving. There are two types of moving violations: waivable and non-waivable. With waivable violations, you can waive the court requirements by admitting guilt and paying the fine. On non-waivable, you must show up for court. These are generally more serious moving violations, such as reckless driving or driving more than 25 mph above the speed limit. Another type of non-waivable violation, for which you must attend court, is if you have received more than three tickets in the previous 12 months.

Moving violations

Moving violations are issued when an officer finds fault with the way you are operating your vehicle. This could include, for example, speeding, running a traffic signal, or failing to signal. When you receive a moving violation ticket and committed a non-waivable violation, you will be instructed to sign your name at the bottom. This is a contract that you will appear in court at the date and time the ticket states. Signing your name on the ticket does not indicate you are confessing your guilt.

Many people do not understand they must appear in court on that date. They mistakenly believe that signing the ticket only serves as an acknowledgement they have received the ticket. As mentioned in Chapter 1, if you do not show up for court, in many states the judge can issue a bench warrant for failing to appear and your license could be suspended without further notification.

Non-moving violations

Non-moving violations are far less serious and do not damage your driving record. These are things such as parking and re-pair tickets.

Types of Speed Limits

- The "85th Percentile Rule"
- Absolute speed limit

- Presumed, or *prima facie*, speed limit

- Basic speed law

The 85th Percentile Rule

When deciding what speed limit to set for a particular road, traffic engineers sometimes use a rule of thumb called the "85th Percentile Rule." This standard comes from numerous studies, which conclusively show the safest speed to drive is the speed 85 percent of the people on the road are traveling at, or below, on any road, when the driving conditions are normal. These studies also show that most people drive at a speed they feel is safe for the current conditions. This may be higher than the posted speed limit. One source that supports this is **www.fairtrafficlaws.com/Speed_ and_Driving_Safely.html**. No state has enacted this rule and none follow it as a law. This is only a general guideline for traffic engineers. Once they set the speed limit based on the rule, that is the speed limit. You cannot successfully defend yourself in court by stating, "Yes, the speed limit was 45 mph, but about 85 percent of other drivers were traveling at 85 mph." However, you may be able to successfully defend that you were driving safely because you felt most safe going the average speed of other drivers.

Absolute speed limits

An absolute speed limit means the speed limit posted is the only speed limit. If you drive one mile per hour over, you can be ticketed. If you live in a state where absolute speed limits are on the books, your defenses are truly quite limited. You need to prove the officer was wrong in the way he or she clocked your speed or that there was some type of life-threatening emergency. Whichever one you choose, you will need to have a strong defense ready.

Presumed speed limits

Presumed speed limits are a little more complicated, but do offer you more flexibility when mounting your defense. Every state's exact wording differs, but they all essentially break down like this: There is a posted speed limit, but if your driving speed is reasonable for the traffic and road conditions and it does not endanger anyone, you can often get away with it. Legally, the posted speed limit is presumed to be the highest safe speed. You can circumvent the speed law by claiming you were not speeding, like you can in an "absolute speed" case. "Presumed speed limit" states recognize it can be safe to exceed the posted limit and allow defendants to prove they were acting with care. It is important to note, however, because the speed limit gives rise to a presumption that your speed was unsafe, the burden of proving otherwise rests on you.

This is not to say that simply telling the judge it is your right to speed as long as you are safe is going to work and ensure your acquittal. Rather, you will need to present actual evidence that your speed was safe. This could include evidence about road conditions that day, what speed other cars typically travel on that road and the time of day, information about how busy the road was, and weather conditions.

For example, if you can prove you were driving 75 mph in a 60 mph zone on a clear Sunday morning at 6 a.m., with no other traffic on the road, you may have a viable defense. Although you were speeding, you were driving safely. Under these circumstances, it would be difficult for the prosecution to prove you were not driving safely. There are many roads across the country that are straight and wide-open. Nonetheless, these roads could have a posted speed limit of 30 mph. In the United States, speeds can go up to 80 miles per hour.

If you are pulled over during clear weather with excellent visibility and the traffic is relatively light, a judge may find you not guilty, even if you were speeding. Do not be discouraged if there was quite a bit of traffic at the time you were stopped for speeding. As you will see later in this book, the presence of more traffic can also work in your favor if it allows you to question whether the officer pulled over the right car.

It can be difficult to figure out whether your state follows the "presumed" or the "absolute" speed limit laws. When you are doing your legal research, you can look for a few key phrases. If you read the law and it mentions it is "unlawful to exceed" or "no person shall drive in excess of," then your state likely has an absolute speed limit. On the other hand, if your law reads that it is "lawful to drive below the posted speed limit in the absence of an obvious hazard" or "prima facie unlawful to exceed," but it does not outright forbid driving over the speed limit, then you most likely live in a presumed speed limit state.

Basic speed limits

The basic speed limit is the third type of speed limit, and every state has this. The basic speed law says that you can be ticketed for speeding — even if you are driving under the posted speed limit — if you are driving too fast or too slow for current road and weather conditions. Regardless of whether a state abides by an "absolute speed limit" or a "presumed speed limit," you can still be ticketed for violating the "basic speed law."

When arguing a basic speed limit ticket, the state must prove you were driving unsafely. As stated before, this can be difficult to do. Officers tend to rely on the basic speed limit statute when you have been involved in an accident. Officers could try to use the accident itself as proof you were driving too fast for conditions. If the officer does testify the accident was a result of you driving at an unsafe speed for the conditions, you must be prepared to challenge the officer's testimony. You could do this by proving that the accident would have happened anyway, given the erratic driving of another party involved.

If there is no accident, but the officer cites you for violating the basic speed law, then he or she must testify under oath that based on the weather, traffic, or road conditions, your speed was still too fast, even though you were driving under the posted speed limit. This can be difficult for an officer to legitimately do.

To develop the most effective defense in a traffic case, you truly do need to spend some time doing legal research. It is to your benefit to figure out what type of speed limit is in effect in your state and the exact wording of the statute you were charged under. Keep meticulous notes because you will need them later.

CHAPTER 3

Should You Fight Your Ticket or Pay?

Sometimes, it is hard to decide whether you should fight a traffic ticket or pay it. Fighting it can take time and effort on your part, but it could end up saving you money — both immediately and in years to come.

If you choose to just pay it, there will be zero time commitment. However, you will pay court costs, the actual fines, plus increased insurance rates. The increased insurance rates could last for several years.

Should you be stopped a second time, if you have automatically paid the first ticket, it will immediately show up on your driving record. The next officer who stops you will see it and you are much more likely to get another ticket if you already have one on your record. Some drivers, like Cynthia Reeser, have changed their driving patterns due to an excessive number of traffic tickets. People like Reeser will tell you to fight your ticket, but try to avoid getting a ticket altogether.

CASE STUDY: TRAFFIC TICKETS HELPED TO CHANGE MY DRIVING PATTERNS

Cynthia Reeser
Editor and Writer
www.prickofthespindle.com

Cynthia Reeser is an editor and writer active in online publishing. She is the author of *How to Publish Your Children's Book: Everything You Need to Know Explained Simply*, and her book on Kindle publishing is forthcoming in 2010.

A former military staff writer and book review columnist, her nonfiction, poetry, and book reviews can be found in various publications, both print and online. She is a chronic speeder who forces herself to drive the speed limit.

Nobody likes traffic tickets. They add points against your driver license and can send insurance rates up. If you feel you have received a speeding ticket in error, it is important to take the time to appear on the assigned court date to contest the fine. Even if you are uncertain you will win, appearing can be well worth the effort. If you lose, take the driving course — they are almost always cheaper than paying the ticket, and the satisfactory completion will result in no points added to your record.

It is important to observe the speed limits. Even if you feel they should be higher, they are in place for a reason. Many people are impatient drivers, myself included. When I received one too many traffic tickets, I had to change my driving habits. Sometimes that means driving the speed limit even when others are going around you. It has been my experience that even when I was driving with the flow of traffic, I was still fined, even though everyone else was speeding. Do not give the police a reason to pull you over. Go the speed limit, observe all the traffic laws, and in the long run, it will save you money and points on your record.

Do periodic safety checks of your vehicle. A police officer can pull you over for something as small as a brake light that is out, or of course for something more serious, like an expired tag. Like any driving course instructor will tell you, driving is a privilege, not a right. Attend to vehicle maintenance on a regular basis, and treat driving like the privilege it is, and it will cost you less in the long run.

Understanding the Negative Effects of Traffic Tickets

There are many negative consequences of getting a traffic ticket. These include fines, increased insurance rates, and in some cases, license suspensions. So you can fully appreciate these possible consequences, take a look at them more closely.

Fines

As addressed in the preface to this book, traffic tickets bring in big revenues through the fines they impose. The average ticket is around $150.

States make it truly easy for you to pay your fines. You will receive a self-addressed envelope with your ticket and often a link to a Web site to pay it through. They do this because it costs them time and money if you fight your ticket. While paying the ticket can sometimes seem the easiest alternative, a minor traffic infraction will linger on your record for up to three years, while an alcohol-related offense can stay there even longer.

Insurance rates

Depending on your insurance company, your rates may go up if you have had just one traffic infraction in a series of years. Much of this depends on where you live and who your insurance agent is. This may be one of your considerations when deciding whether to pay this ticket. Thinking about insurance consequences makes you think twice about just paying the first ticket and forgetting about it. Beyond the financial ramifications of one or multiple traffic tickets, you risk losing your license when you rack up too many points and citations.

Another plus to fighting a ticket, in regards to your insurance rates, is that some insurance companies offer you incentives for staying ticket free. These can include reduced deductible rates and rebate checks. Over time, these incentives can add up.

While you might not feel the immediate impact of a single traffic ticket as it relates to your insurance rates, you could be setting yourself up for a bigger hit later. It is worth considering.

License suspensions

Getting your license suspended is a result of receiving more than one ticket in a specific period of time. However, there are exceptions to this generalized rule and they are as follows:

- You are under 18 years of age, in some states.

- You are charged with any alcohol-related offense, criminal speeding, or vehicular manslaughter.

If either of these applies to your current situation, you are potentially looking at an immediate suspension of your license regardless of how long it has been since you had a traffic ticket.

Most license suspensions are directly related to the Department of Motor Vehicles' "point system." The specifics of the system are different depending on what state you have your license in, but the basic rules are the same. Each driving infraction carries a specified point value. If you are convicted of a driving infraction, those points are "added" to your license.

For minors, most states require fewer points before suspending a license. In Georgia, for example, a driver under the age of 18 is only allowed four points before the state can suspend his or her license. This means a minor driver could potentially lose his or her license on the first offense, if that offense carried four or more points.

On the other side of the points issue, for every year that you are infraction-free, points are "subtracted" from your driver's license. So, there are people out there with "negative" points on their license, which is a good thing.

For example, a woman in Maine has not had a traffic ticket in five years. Therefore, in the state of Maine, she currently has negative five points on her license. If she were to be convicted on a speeding charge that carried a point value of "two," she would then have negative three points on her license. You can find the relevant point system for your state in the online Unofficial DMV Guide at: **www.dmv.org/point-system.php**.

Most insurance companies will figure the amount of points on your license when calculating your rate. As a general rule of thumb, minor infractions will result in a rate increase for ten to 12 months. More serious offenses, however, can result in rate increases in excess of that period. Find more information about this in an article published by *Ezine Articles* in September 2008. Visit **http://ezinearticles.com** and search for the article titled "How Long is a Speeding Ticket Held Against You For Auto Insurance Purposes?"

You might be asking, "Is there a way to reduce the points on my license that are already sitting there, costing me extra money?" While this book was not designed to give you advice on ridding points once you have them, it ties in with another "fighting your ticket" topic: traffic school.

Traffic school

Just as it sounds, traffic school is a place you go to learn the rules of the road — or re-learn if for some reason you have forgotten them. Attending traffic school will sometimes give you a "credit" of up to three points on your driver's license.

In most states, traffic school will wipe your current ticket off your record. It also means you will not risk increased insurance rates because of the ticket. If you choose not to fight your ticket and would rather just pay it, ask about traffic school. Some states limit the amount of times an individual can take traffic school.

Alternative options to going to a physical traffic school location are online versions and a take-home version available at many video-rental stores. Online courses can cost between $25 and $50 and take-home versions vary in price by location. Visit Traffic School Online at **http://trafficschoolonline.com**. Weigh these costs of paying the ticket and paying for the class against possible costs from fighting the ticket in court. Remember: If you plead guilty to your ticket and traffic school is mandated within the sentence you receive, you will still be assessed the points and could see an increased insurance rate.

When it comes to deciding whether to fight a traffic ticket, it is truly a personal choice. You need to logically weigh the information you have, what you know about the law you have been charged under, the evidence you can collect to refute it, and the time investment it will take to mount the defense. If you feel you have a chance, then by all means fight it. You have nothing to lose.

Here are some possible questions to consider when making a decision:

- Are you sure the officer correctly clocked your speed? How did he or she clock you? What are some of your possible defenses to the method he or she used?

- Did you actually clock the speed of your vehicle? How many other makes and models look similar to what you were driving at the time of the stop? Was traffic heavy when you were stopped? Is it possible that he or she could have clocked your car and then lost you in the sea of rush hour traffic? If you were issued a ticket from a traffic camera at an intersection, were you the one actually driving the vehicle at the time?

- Where was the officer parked? When he or she clocked you, was there anything blocking his or her direct line of vision? This includes construction equipment or public services vehicles parked in the median. During the winter, think about the height of snow banks.

- What kind of speed limit does your state have — presumed or absolute?

Commercial Truck Drivers

A special note for semi-truck drivers or anyone who has a commercial license: Regardless of what you are charged with, consult with an attorney before you pay any ticket you receive. Those who hold a commercial driver's license often drive hundreds of thousands of miles each year, much of them outside their home states. Not only are semi-truck drivers held to a higher standard than a driver with a non-commercial license, they also have much more on the line. Where a minor traffic ticket may have small consequences for an individual without a commercial license, it can carry serious criminal and civil repercussions for a truck driver.

Your livelihood depends on your driver's license being in good standing. Therefore, you should fight each ticket you receive; even a minor traffic citation can have a major impact on the status of your commercial driver's license.

There are several serious commercial driver's license violations, which include:

- Speeding 15 mph or over the posted speed limit

- Reckless driving

- Improper lane change

- Following another vehicle too closely

- Any accident involving a fatality

- Failing to stop or slow down at a railroad crossing

- No commercial driver's license in possession

Your commercial driver's license can be affected in a number of ways when you get a traffic citation. While one infraction is not likely to deprive you of a license, it can cause your insurance rates to go up. If you are a solo driver, and thus an owner-operator, you will personally pay the increased fees.

Consequences of traffic tickets for commercial drivers vary from state to state. While the federal government imposes minimum standards relating to trucking, each state has the ability to expand on those rules slightly. State-by-state information on commercial trucking standards can be found in the online "Unofficial DMV Guide" at **www.dmv.org/commercial-license.php**.

If you drive for a company, your employer might not like the idea of having to pay more in insurance rates because you got a ticket. In some states, like Maine, the company employing the truck driver receives the same ticket when an individual commercial driver receives a traffic infraction.

The most common commercial driving infraction handed out is a logbook violation. As a commercial driver, you are only allowed to drive a certain amount of hours per day and per week. Currently, federal law caps that at 11 hours a day, with a ten-hour rest period following. Your logbook tracks every stop you make, how far you have driven, and how many hours you have driven each day. Commercial truck driving is often a low-paying job, therefore many drivers are tempted to "cheat" on their logbooks. Do not do this, as it is not worth the fine.

CHAPTER 4

How the Police Measure Your Speed

As you know, there are a variety of ways in which you can be caught speeding. Police officers use many different methods to catch speed violators. Some of these methods are not legal in all 50 states, so it is a good idea to research what is and what is not legal.

There are six ways to get caught speeding:

- Visual estimates

- Pacing

- Timing

- VASCAR

- Radar

- Air patrol

- Photo radar

Visual Estimates

This is when an officer looks at a car and takes an educated guess as to how fast it is traveling. This is one of the least scientific ways to catch a speeder and often the easiest one to fight. There are few officers who will pull a driver over simply based on a visual estimate. If an officer sees you and thinks you are speeding, he or she will try to pace you.

Pacing

There are many tickets that are issued based on an officer pacing a driver. If you ever see a police officer following you at a consistent distance for any length of time, he or she is likely pacing you to see if you are speeding.

For an accurate measure of your speed, an officer must "pace" you by keeping an equal distance between his or her car and yours for the entire time you are being watched. This can be done while he or she is in front of you or behind you, so be aware. Pacing is a tricky task and requires special training for the officer to effectively measure your speed. It requires that he or she "bumper pace" your car, meaning the officer needs to keep a constant distance between his or her front bumper and your back bumper.

As you can well imagine, this proves to be more difficult the farther back the officer is. In addition, many things can throw off the reading, including upgrades, downgrades, and curves in the roadway. Some states also require an officer pace you over a certain distance. If you notice that a police car is directly behind you, then falls back, then pops up again in your mirrors, it is a good indicator that he or she is not accurately pacing you, and you can effectively mount a defense in court.

For example, a play-by-play of how pacing works. You will notice the police car beginning to follow you, and then you will see that it is close to your bumper. The more distance the police have to cover, the faster you will notice the police car bearing down on you. There is a mathematical equation to figure out the distance between where the officer initially started and the distance that your car traveled after the police car started following you.

Your speed will equal the officer's speed, divided by one plus the initial distance the officer's car was behind you, divided by the distance your car traveled before the officer caught up to you. In numbers, it looks like this:

Officer's speed = 80 mph/ (1+ (.5 miles behind you/2 miles you drove))

Your speed = 64 mph

There are obvious problems with pacing. The lay of the land can cause huge problems with this form of speed enforcement. The presence of hills, curves, and traffic intersections can all help in your defense when it comes to refuting a claim that an officer paced you — especially if your state mandates that a driver be paced for a specific distance. Imagine the ability of an officer to pace you properly when he or she cannot even see your car for the entire time due to peaks and valleys.

Another problem with pacing can be the police car's speedometer. In order to check a patrol car's speedometer request discovery and be sure to ask for a copy of the police car's maintenance records. The speedometer is required to be calibrated once a year — if it is not, the reading could be inaccurate. The burden of proof lies with the state when it comes to the accuracy of the officer's speedometer — but only if the defendant brings it up. *How to request discovery will be discussed later in Chapter 9.*

Likewise, it is difficult for a police officer to pace a driver at dusk and twilight hours, and pacing simply does not work in the sheer dark of night. If an officer paces you with only your taillights as proof, chances are it will be an easy ticket to fight. However, few officers will use this as a legitimate speed enforcement tool during nighttime hours.

VASCAR

VASCAR — short for Visual Average Speed Computer and Recorder — sounds technical, and it is. Fortunately for you, it also requires hands-on input from the police officer, which means it is far more likely to have errors in its findings.

VASCAR is like a stopwatch embedded into a computer program. To use VASCAR, an officer must first measure the distance between two stationary points. He or she can do this using his or her car's odometer or measuring tape. The car's odometer is connected to the VASCAR program in the computer, so officers normally use that.

When an officer sees a car she suspects is speeding, she pushes a button on the computer to start the VASCAR program's electronic stopwatch as the car meets the first stationary point. When the car passes the second point, the officer pushes the button again. The end result is a reading telling the officer how fast the car is moving.

Officers can use the VASCAR program while sitting idle or while they are moving. When they are moving, the VASCAR unit is programmed to take into account that the police car is moving while following you. Overall, there are four different ways in which officers use the VASCAR:

- **While parked,** after measuring the distance of two set points with either measuring tape or the car's odometer.

- **While following you and manually telling the VASCAR unit that his or her car is moving too.** This particular method involves a lot of button pushing, as the officer must push the "time" switch when you pass her predetermined point, and then the "distance" switch as you pass the same point. When you pass the second point, she must push the "time" switch a second time and also the "distance" switch a second time to mark her passing the second stationary point. That is a lot of buttons for anyone to push, and it equates to more when the officer is trying to drive while he or she does it.

- **While driving ahead of you.** This involves the officer watching you in her rear-view mirror, and hitting the time button twice as she sees you pass both set points. Again, this involves the officer not only paying attention to the traffic ahead of her, but also watching what you are doing behind her and being sure to push the "time" switch at two precise moments.

- **While driving toward you in the opposite direction.** This is a little more tricky, but involves the officer hitting the "time" button on the VASCAR unit as you pass one predetermined point, and then hitting it again as you pass his or her car, essentially setting the second point. This is often what has happened when you see a police officer complete a U-turn and pull you over.

You may be able to point out a number of ways the VASCAR system can fail both the officers and the drivers they are pulling over. Yet, it is a preferred method of tracking speeding because it is much more flexible than its "pacing" counterpart. This is because the officer does not have to worry about how fast she is going, as long as she is sure to hit the right buttons at the right time.

That said, it is not easy to manipulate all those buttons, especially if someone is trying to drive at the same time. The VASCAR program itself is truly a good tool in speed enforcement. However, basic human errors can cause more frustration and traffic tickets than it is worth.

If your speed was measured by VASCAR, ask yourself some important questions when determining how you will approach your defense.

- How did the officer track you?

- Was she sitting in a stationary spot or driving at the same time?

- How far away was her car parked from her two chosen measuring points? Did she have a clear line of vision?

- Remember, the farther away the officer was sitting, the more likely it is that she could misjudge when you passed the marker. What about her reaction time?

Scientists have concluded that it takes more than three-tenths of a second to react to something that is just 18 inches in front of someone. The shorter the distance between two points, the quicker a car will pass both, leaving the officer little time to accurately record your time. The same holds true when an officer is far away from her target; except now you must figure in her sight line and the angle at which she sits in relation to the two points.

The National Motorists Association of Waunakee, Wisconsin, published a study by Kenneth A. Moore of JAG Engineering in Manassas, Virginia, titled "An Error Analysis of VASCAR-Plus." Moore has taken the time to compile numerous calculations, charts, and graphs. The final product conclusively shows that VASCAR is prone to errors when the distance between the two points is more than 1,500 or less than 500 feet.

To further add validity to the study, Pennsylvania lawmakers passed a law that forbids a VASCAR speeding conviction if the posted speed limit is less than 55 mph and the readout on the VASCAR unit is not more than 10 mph over the limit. For example, in Pennsylvania, you cannot be convicted based on a VAS-CAR reading for driving 34 mph in a 25 mph zone.

There are many inaccuracies that VASCAR can present. Be sure to bring these up at trial. Do not be afraid to question things, such as the officer's reaction time. Use scientific facts about reaction times to back up your line of questioning. Here are some other key points to consider:

- Where the officer was sitting at the time you were clocked with VASCAR. The farther away the officer sits, the more difficult it is to accurately judge when a car is passing a stationary point. While the officer may be sitting perfectly aligned with the first starting point, he or she certainly cannot be directly in line with the second, and therefore, his or her perception is skewed.

- The officer's reaction time. This has already been covered in detail, but you truly need to keep this in the forefront of your mind. Remember: The closer the two points are together, the less likely it is that the officer will have ample time to accurately record you passing both predetermined points.

- The accuracy of the police car's odometer. A VASCAR unit is directly linked to both a car's odometer and speedometer via a cable. As the car moves, the cable moves too, telling the VASCAR unit the distance and the speed at which the police car is traveling. Therefore, if the odometer or the speedometer is not accurate, the VASCAR unit may not display an accurate reading. There are many things that can affect the accuracy of each of these, including tire pressure and wear.

VASCAR is characteristically used when air patrol is enforcing the speed limits; this is regularly on major highways and thruways. This form of speed enforcement is marginal for several reasons. The air patrolman uses the VASCAR unit to measure your speed between two stationary points, just like ground patrolmen do. But the problem is that groundspeed and airspeed are two very different things. In addition, when the air patrolman clocks you, he sends a description of your car to ground patrol through the patrol radios and the ground patrol officer must find you. Many other cars on the road probably look similar to yours.

Chances are, that the moment you see a ground patrol car speeding up behind you to get a "pace" on your speed, you are going to slow down. If you did slow down and you still got a ticket, challenge that in court. This is especially true if he issues a ticket not off the "pacing" from the ground patrol, but simply off the reading from air patrol. When you choose to fight an air patrol

VASCAR ticket, both police officers must show up. If they do not, the case is thrown out. If they do both show up, request that when one is testifying, the other one leave the courtroom. This decreases the chance that one's memory will be jogged by the other's testimony and it also increases the chance they will contradict each other.

Police will tout the accuracy of VASCAR, and they use it quite frequently. In fact, a Department of Transportation study found that VASCAR is accurate within 2 mph of the driver's actual speed 95 percent of the time. Consequently it is up to you to refute the accuracy and bring up the obvious problems that can occur. Do your research if you were clocked with VASCAR, as it is well worth your time to be "up to speed."

Radar

This tool is used in a large number of speeding cases every day because radar infractions produce the most revenue for the least amount of overhead costs. If you look at the statistics, there are more radar citations handed out than any other kind. Pennsylvania is the only state that does not allow local police to use radar guns.

Two types of radar units are used in speed enforcement: car-mounted and handheld radar units. The car-mounted varieties are frequently mounted on the outside of the back window, on the driver's side. These are hard to see because they are not big and if you are already driving, you probably cannot keep track of a moving police car to see if something is sticking out of the back window. If you see a police car parked in the median, you already know the officer is clocking speeds. If he or she is driving in traffic, you have no idea what the officer is up to.

Car-mounted radar units can be used whether the officer is stationary or moving. The speed read by the beams shows up on a console or dash-mounted device.

Handheld radar units look like plastic guns and, while they can be discreetly tucked in bushes or down next to the officer's leg, they can also be extremely obvious — especially if the officer is standing at the side of the road and pointing it at oncoming traffic. Motorcycle officers most often use handheld radar guns. Officers who stand on the side of the road and clock drivers also use these radar guns. Then they call officers farther down the road to let them know who should be pulled over.

While radar seems flawless, it is far from being an easy conviction in the courtroom. There are many aspects that affect the accuracy of a radar reading, and few of them have to do with human error:

- Radio transmitters and towers cause radar interference

- Citizen Band radios, found in police cars and semi-trucks, can distort radar speed-readings

- Neon lights, power transformers, and electrical storms can interfere with radar speed-readings

- If an officer is using "moving" radar speed-readings and he accelerates too quickly, the radar often does not adjust immediately, causing a misread

- On a windy day, radar can pick up the speed of anything from blowing leaves to rain or dust

In addition, there are other important things to know about radar. For example, for an accurate reading of your speed, the radar beam must be pointed straight at your car. The farther away you are from the radar, the wider the beam becomes and the more likely it is your speed is not what is being picked up. At a distance of just one-eighth of a mile, the beam from a radar unit is the measure of four lanes wide. That leaves a lot of room for it to pick up the car that just went speeding past you. In other words, unless the cop is right on top of you, question the distance.

Radar beams tend to pick up the speeds of larger objects as opposed to smaller ones. So, if you are driving in a sea of cars, the cop may have picked up someone else's speed. Also, consider this: How often have you seen a police officer on the side of the road who quickly raises his arm to clock your speed? Because the officer has to pull the trigger to clock you on radar, if he pushes that button before he is done moving his arm, the radar will pick up the speed of the officer's moving arm in addition to whatever car the beam lands on. It can add an additional eight to ten miles per hour to your speed. How quickly the officer's arm is moving may affect your ticket.

Also, if you were pulled over with a group of cars, ask for the officer's notes during discovery. On many occasions, you will find that the officer clocked the "lead" car and then visually estimated whether there was any change in the distance between that car and the bumpers of the cars behind it. If you are driving on the road at or below the speed limit and a car comes speeding up behind your car, you might get tagged just because you were ahead of a car that was actually speeding.

When fighting a radar citation in court, there are a few things the judge will consider when deciding whether to dismiss your case. Your primary defense will be to question whether the radar unit is accurate; you can do this by requesting the units. Ask for the radar unit's calibration records, maintenance records, the officer's radar training certificate, and verification that the unit has been registered with the Federal Communication Commission (FCC). This is a lot of paperwork, but there are reasons that you will ask for them.

In many states, police officers do not have to be certified or licensed to operate a radar unit. It certainly helps an officer's case if he is certified, but it helps your case if he is not. Verify that the unit itself is registered with the FCC. Because new radar units come into the police departments on a regular basis, it is easy to forget to register them. This does not excuse the fact that each one must be registered before being put into the rotation for speed enforcement use. A radar unit is technically considered a "scientific instrument" that is used for measuring, so it needs to be regularly calibrated to ensure its accuracy. The radar unit can be

calibrated two ways: with a tuning fork, which is the most accurate way, but also the most time-consuming method, or manually, by turning on the "calibrate" or "test" switch that is built in
to the radar unit itself. This indicates whether the instrument is
properly calibrating. The tester reads the signal of an internal fre-
quency-generating device called a crystal. If the unit is correctly
working, it will read out a pre-specified number.

The manual method of testing is less time consuming, but it does
cause many more problems. There are actually two types of circuits inside the radar unit, so both must be tested if the officer
wants to ensure that the unit is indeed properly working. However, the manual method tests only one circuit — the "counting
circuits." In Connecticut, it was decided, via *State v. Tomanelli*,
216 A.2d 625 (1965) that using a certified tuning fork is the scien-
tifically accepted method of calibrating a radar unit.

Furthermore, in the state of Florida, Judge Alfred Nesbitt had this
to say after hearing all arguments and testimony in *State v. Aquil-
era* 48 Fla. Supp. 207, which dealt with the following inherent errors the radar has: "...Cosine error; Batching error; Panning and
Scanning errors; Shadowing errors; errors due to outside interference such as billboards, overpasses, passing [citizen band] radios,
and many other similar causes; errors due to inside interference
such as heaters and air conditioning fans, and police radios etc;
errors due to improper mounting of the radar unit; errors due
to heat buildup; errors due to power surge by shutting off and
turning on the radar at the last minute to avoid radar detecting
devices; errors due to the auto lock system; errors due to reliance

on the auto alarm system; errors due to the mirror switch aiming; and errors in the identification of target vehicles due to the modern-day traffic patterns and the mixture of size of vehicles and varied materials in their construction."

In its decision, the court stated, "Based upon all of the testimony, exhibits, and arguments of counsel, I find that the reliability of the radar speed measuring devices as used in their present modes and particularly in these cases, has not been established beyond and to the exclusion of every reasonable doubt, nor has it met the test of reasonable scientific certainty, and it is therefore ordered and adjudged that the motions to suppress and/or exclude herein be and they are hereby granted."

So far, this chapter has covered pacing, visual estimating, VAS-CAR, and radar − but there is more. So, while the previously mentioned methods are by far the most popular to track a driver's speed, there is yet another out there: the laser. You have likely heard about it, but maybe you do not know the details, so take a look.

Laser

Also known as "lidar," this is shortened terminology for Light Detection and Ranging or Laser Speed Measuring Device. It uses three low-powered beams of laser light that bounce off targeted cars and returns to the receiver in the unit. The unit electronically calculates the speed of the targeted vehicles.

While laser is supposed to be far more accurate than a radar unit, it is not the choice of speed enforcement technology that most police officers choose. While the three very thin beams of light significantly reduce the risk of clocking another car and making an erroneous stop, these three beams must all be held on the targeted vehicle at the same time for the reading to be accurate. Not only that, but it is impossible to verify that it has been done correctly since the beams are invisible. Also, and because it uses light to measure speed, it can be ineffective on cars that are dark in color.

Air Patrol

In case you skipped over the VASCAR section because you were caught speeding by air patrol, go back to that section. Air patrol uses VASCAR to time your speed between two predetermined points; then a ground patrol officer has the responsibility of issuing you a ticket.

Photo Radar

Finally, photo radar is the last of the methods police officers can employ catch you speeding. The use of photo radar appeared in the United States more than a decade ago, but has been used for almost three decades in Europe.

Just as it sounds, this is a radar unit that takes pictures. Frequently tucked on the side of the road, the camera unit is not obvious. This particular radar unit has a computer attached, which is programmed to trigger the camera when a car exceeds a certain speed

limit. The camera then takes a picture of the front of the car, ide-
ally capturing both the front license plate and the driver's face.

Sometimes it does not happen so perfectly. When the photos are
developed, the license plates are often illegible or you cannot see
the driver's face. If the license plate is legible, the police will run
the plate and send the ticket in the mail. Always request the photos from the camera if you receive one of these tickets. You will
need to verify that the driver's face is identifiable. If you cannot
see who the driver is, the state has no way to prove you were the
one who was speeding; for all they know, your friend borrowed
your car that day.

A few other texts, which deal with fighting traffic tickets, recommend just ignoring these types of tickets as they come in the
mail and are commonly not certified. Some authors' take on it
is: No one can verify that you received the ticket in the mail, so
you do not have to acknowledge it. The other argument is since
you did not sign the ticket, you certainly did not promise to appear in court.

However, you should never intentionally ignore a citation. If you
have a defense, then schedule a court date and fight the ticket.
Photo radar cameras are highly controversial because of the inaccuracy, so it should not be a hard fight to win.

CHAPTER 5

The Different Types
of Moving Violations

More often than not, if you are going to get a traffic ticket, it is going to be a speeding ticket, but not all moving violations involve speeding. Although the majority of this book has addressed speed violations thus far, you do need to learn about the other moving violations that can occur. These violations are treated as petty offenses or violations. A petty offense is a type of misdemeanor. Typically, they carry low fines and are not punishable with jail time. Traditionally, petty offenses are heard before a magistrate judge in a summary proceeding, without the right to a jury trial. Violations, on the other hand, are not considered part of criminal law, but are treated like petty offenses: heard before a magistrate and limited due process rights. In many cases, these moving violations involve a "judgment call" on behalf of the officer. Luckily, tickets that rely on a judgment call are often beaten in court.

Failure to Stop

This means that you did not stop your vehicle where you should have — this may be at a stop sign or traffic light. If you run straight through or even roll through it, you can be issued a ticket. In driver's training, instructors teach you to pull up, count to three, and then proceed.

But a stop is a stop, right? Most statutes read that you have to stop at the "limit line," which is that white line painted on the road several feet in front of the stop sign and, more often than not, before the pedestrian cross walk. If there is no limit line but there is a crosswalk, then the crosswalk serves as the limit line.

You stopped before the limit line

Some drivers are extra careful and likely stop before the limit line. If an officer is sitting on a side street and does not have a clear view of the road you are driving on, it is quite likely that he may think you did not stop at all. If you come back into his line of sight, you will be accelerating through the stop sign. To be able to mount a defense, it is critical that you request a copy of the officer's notes. After you get them, head back to the scene of the citation and sit in your car, exactly where the officer said he was sitting. Take pictures from his vantage point, and use those to prove in court that the officer could not have possibly seen you stop prior to the limit line because of where he was stationed.

Obstructions of view

There are other instances where you can justify rolling through a stop sign. Tree branches frequently fall down during or after a storm. It is possible one was obstructing your view of the sign. It is also possible that someone twisted the sign around, so you could not see it at all. If you have pictures to back these things up, they will be helpful in court.

The officer thought your light was red

Sometimes, traffic lights are improperly synchronized. When this happens, the light turns green for the waiting traffic before the other direction turns red. While this is dangerous and should be brought to the attention of the city, that does not help you if you have already received the ticket. If an officer is sitting at an inter-section you drive through because your light is green or yellow, and his light turns green before you are through, chances are he will ticket you. The officer will think you ran the red light, but that does not mean you did.

Go back to the intersection and get documentation that the light was mistimed. You can do this through video or statements given by other motorists. Do not be afraid to approach people and tell them what you are looking for. You will be surprised how many of them would be willing to testify to the light's minor malfunc-tion. Not only will it help a fellow motorist, it will bring much-needed attention to the problem so the city can fix the timing and prevent future accidents.

CASE STUDY: I FOUGHT MY TRAFFIC TICKET FOR RUNNING A RED LIGHT AND WON

Jeanne Worrick
www.sellikeagirl.com

I have been a sales representative in the commercial/industrial oil industry for the past 20 years, and I travel on the road almost every day, putting more miles on my car than the average person. Therefore, I have a greater chance of receiving a ticket, but a traffic ticket can have a devastating effect on my business. In Massachusetts, if a driver receives three moving violations within 12 months, the driver's license can be revoked. I have had several traffic tickets over the years, mostly for speeding.

The experience I had when I fought a ticket and won was years ago when I was stopped at a red light near my home, on a road that I traveled daily. The light was red for way too long and I knew this light had experienced malfunctions before. There was a police officer behind me, but after waiting at this light for an extended period, I slowly and cautiously drove through it. Sure enough, the officer turned on his blue light and pulled me over to the side of the road. He gave me a hard time about going through the red light, so I explained my reasoning. He told me the light turned green right after I drove through it. I apologized and again explained my reasoning, but he gave me a ticket and I went to the District Court to state my case.

Before I went to court, I called the local police station and asked about that specific traffic light. I got a police officer to agree the light always had problems, and I asked if I could use his name in court. He agreed. When I went before the judge, I simply told him my story honestly and quoted this police officer from the station who corroborated my story of the light being in poor working order on many occasions. The judge ruled in my favor.

I encourage you to fight your traffic ticket if you believe you have a strong case.

Red light cameras

These seem to be popping up everywhere. Some cities use the cameras to catch red light runners, while other cities use them to have documentation of what happened in the moments leading up to and during an accident. No doubt, these cameras have helped the police sort out dozens of accidents. However, these cameras may not be good at detecting and accurately ticketing drivers who run red lights. Similar to the photo radar, these cameras are set up to snap a shot of the vehicle's front license plate and the driver, when a sensor in the intersection is triggered. If a motorist runs a red light, the local police department writes the person a ticket and sends it through standard mail.

In most states that use these red light cameras, the law states that the driver, not the vehicle's owner, is liable for the ticket. An officer is required to look at each of the tickets to be sure there was no mistake. In theory, citizens can fight their tickets by filling out an affidavit, swearing that he or she was not driving at the time, and they will not have to pay the ticket.

Unfortunately, red light cameras do not always work very well. The cameras generate a large volume of tickets and few officers on staff are commissioned to verify them. In 2008, for example, the City of Los Angeles issued more than 30,000 tickets at 32 camera-equipped intersections. Many tickets in many cities slip through the cracks and are mailed out. As a result, errors occur quite frequently.

A news station in Seattle, King 5 News, discovered some red light camera inaccuracies in February 2008. Upon investigation, reporters found a local resident who received three of these red light tickets from two different cameras. However, on all three occasions he was cited by the red light camera, he was deployed with the military and serving in Iraq. His father went to court to fight all three tickets. On each ticket, the listed license plate, color of the car, and number of doors on the car all were wrong.

The soldier's car was a two-door silver coupe. The car that had actually been running the red lights was a black, four-door sedan. As a result of the errors the red light cameras make, hundreds of motorists spend countless hours fighting these tickets. This ties up the legal system and is ultimately costly to maintain.

As with photo radar, it is critical to get the photographs from the camera. Examine the pictures to make sure the driver even looks like you and whether the license plate can be clearly read. If not, you have a good chance of getting the ticket thrown out of court. At your trial, the state must provide documentation on how the red light camera works and evidence that it was working properly on the day you were cited. If they do not, again, your case can be dismissed.

Illegal Turns

You have seen these signs everywhere. "No U-turns" and "No Left Hand Turns Between 7 a.m. to 10 a.m." These signs are normally put in place for the sake of keeping traffic moving at a good clip and avoiding congestion during peak driving times. However, many people do risk it and make the illegal turn. The best defense when you receive these tickets is the same as the other infractions: try to prove that you were not driving unsafely.

U-turn in a business district

Many times, U-turns are prohibited in business districts, due to the amount of traffic these areas see. If you do a U-turn and receive a ticket, investigate what your state defines as a "business district." After you look it up, head back to the scene of the citation and see if where you were ticketed actually falls in to the "business district" definition.

U-turn in a residential neighborhood

Receiving a ticket for this offense is not common. U-turns in a residential neighborhood are often allowed as long as there is no oncoming traffic. Even if there is oncoming traffic, a U-turn is legal as long as the traffic is a few hundred feet away. If you receive one of these tickets, look up the exact wording of the statute. If the statute says you cannot make a U-turn in a residential neighborhood when another car is within 250 feet, your best defense is to argue whether the oncoming car was actually within 250 feet.

It can help to use photographs, maps, and diagrams that have a distance scale included. In these cases, it often comes down to your word against the officer's, which is why these tickets are not common.

U-turns on the highway

You have just gone past your exit and you see that ominous sign, "Next exit 25 miles." You quickly weigh your options and realize that, if you drive all the way to the next exit, get off, get back on, and drive back to the exit you need, you are looking at an extra hour's worth of driving time. Not considering the obvious risk of making a U-turn on the highway, you pull the car in to the median and you are back on the right path in no time. The problem? An officer saw you and is now heading straight towards your car.

In some states, the highways are clearly marked and signs read you cannot use the median to make a U-turn. Other states leave it up to the driver's imagination. If you live in a state where U-turns are allowed on the highway, but there are certain restrictions, be sure to read the statute and try to prove that you were within the restrictions. However, if you live in a state that strictly forbids U-turns on the highway and you just got a ticket for making one, you may not be able to argue a defense. You can try to prove you had a dire emergency — for example, if you or your passenger needed emergency medical attention. An officer would rather call an ambulance to the scene than give you a ticket.

U-turns on a raised traffic median/island

Yes, it is true. Some people do actually make a U-turn by going over one of those raised traffic medians. Anyone who does this risks car damage and receiving a ticket.

Do your legal research and find out exactly what the law says, and then start dissecting it. Most states have a provision in their statute about double lines and openings within the traffic medians or barriers that can serve as "driveways." They may talk about the traffic lines that lead up to these "driveways" and how far apart they must be. You can go back and measure these lines to see if the workers painting the lines made a mistake. You can also argue that it appeared there was an opening meant to be a "driveway."

Either way, it will help if you have photos to back up what you are claiming. Your final defense to this type of moving violation is to claim that you had to go over the traffic island to avoid being caught up in a dangerous traffic situation — usually this can be an accident or an out-of-control driver. In this case, the burden of proof rests solely on your shoulders. If you come to court with this defense, you need proof there truly was an emergency.

Unsafe Lane Changes

This category is where undefined traffic offenses go. Basically, a driver cannot move his or her vehicle left or right until that person can do so safely. This can be subjective on the part of the officer. The state has the burden of proving your lane change was unsafe — that is a good thing. Be prepared to show evidence that you were completely safe in your actions.

Some "unsafe lane change" tickets that you could see are as follows:

Turning left with oncoming traffic

If the light is green or you have no signs instructing you to stop, it is legal to make a left-hand turn with oncoming traffic headed your way. However, you must complete the turn with reasonable safety. If an overzealous police officer pulls you over after you have made your turn and gives you a ticket, challenge it in court.

You can start your defense by presenting evidence that your left-handed turn did not cause an accident. You can say that no other drivers had to swerve or slam on their brakes to avoid hitting you. Use diagrams to show where your car was in relation to the oncoming traffic, and use math. Six car lengths equal about 100 feet. How many car lengths were between you and the car that was driving toward you? This ticket is completely subjective on the officer's part and, therefore, incredibly easy to fight.

Pulling out in front of someone

For safety's sake and common courtesy, do not pull out in front of someone unless you have ample time and space. These tickets can also be issued if you change lanes too quickly without signaling your intentions to other drivers.

To argue a ticket for this, you can employ a few techniques in your defense. Use a diagram to demonstrate where your car was in relation to the car you pulled out in front of. Testify that the other driver did not have to swerve and he or she did not slam on his or her brakes to avoid hitting you.

You may also want to bring in to question the officer's line of view and whether it was obstructed at the time the turn was made. Chances are, unless the officer was right behind you or sitting at the intersection, he did not get a good look at what actually happened; he or she subjectively put the pieces together.

Backing down the road

This is not typical driving behavior, but it could happen if another driver simply becomes erratic and you need to pull away from him or her. Road rage by an oncoming driver may also force you to drive backward down a road to get out of his or her path. You should be prepared to honestly prove that another driver's patterns forced you to drive like this. You will likely need other witnesses from the incident to corroborate your testimony of the oncoming driver's erratic behavior.

Failing to signal

These citations are handed out quite frequently. Officers write "fail to signal" tickets when the driver did not signal for at least 100 feet before making his or her turn. Since it is your word against the officer's, these tickets are hard to beat.

The only real defense here is to prove that you did, in fact, signal in time. To prove this, you should testify as to where you started signaling and that your signals were working at the time you received the ticket. Diagrams and photos can help, but corroborating witnesses are the best evidence.

The only chance you have to beat this type of citation is to claim mistake-of-fact, meaning you thought you signaled and therefore, followed the law. If your back light is burned out, you may have a valid defense because you were not aware that the turn signal was not working. You will have to prove you were completely unaware that the bulb was burned out, not just that you were ignoring getting it fixed.

CASE STUDY: I FOUGHT MY TICKET FOR "FAILING TO SIGNAL" AND WON

Alana Cash

There are a few basic, standard rules for fighting a traffic ticket in court.

First, know the law and be prepared to argue it. Second, be serious. Do not be silly, sarcastic, or rude to anyone in the courtroom. Do not raise your voice or whine. Never lie.

I once got a ticket for not using my left-hand turn signal. I was driving on an unlit road alongside a park that had closed for the evening. There was no traffic behind me and no oncoming traffic. When I made the left-hand turn, I did not use the turn signal, as there was no one to signal. I saw the patrol car, which was parked on the wrong side of the road, facing my vehicle as I turned the corner. I passed the patrol car, and the officer turned the vehicle around, flashed the lights, and I stopped. He gave me a ticket for not using the turn signal.

I looked up the law, which stated that the driver of a vehicle must signal a turn 100 feet before the intersection. The law did not state that I had to be signaling during the turn or after the turn. I was mandated to signal before the turn only.

In court, the officer testified that I had come around the corner so quickly that he thought I was going to hit his patrol car. He stated that he noticed I did not have my turn signal on and that is why he gave me a ticket. I asked the officer if he gave me a ticket for reckless driving or for speeding. He said he did not. That answer ensured I was not portrayed as a wild driver.

Then, I asked the officer if he saw any other vehicles on the road behind me or crossing the intersection after I turned. He did not. I asked him if there was a stop sign or a yield sign on the corner of the street where he was parked. He said there was a stop sign. There actually was no sign at all. I asked if he could describe what I was wearing, if I had the radio on, how fast I was going. He did not know.

My argument to the judge was that I only had to signal for 100 feet, and from where the officer was parked, he could not see if I signaled or not. Furthermore, as there were no other cars on the road, who was I signaling? The purpose of giving a signal is to inform other drivers of my intention to turn. If there are no other drivers, I was still practicing safe driving. Finally, I pointed out that the officer was clearly not observant, as he did not even know that there was no sign on the street.

I neither admitted nor denied that I signaled and the prosecutor never asked me. The judge dismissed the ticket — I won the case.

Right-of-Way Violations

These citations are issued when you fail to give another motorist or pedestrian the "right-of-way." A right-of-way is the legal right of a pedestrian or motorist to proceed before you. For example, oncoming traffic has the right to go before someone making a left-hand turn. A pedestrian in a crosswalk usually has the right to cross before any traffic. And, if two cars pull up to a stop sign at the same time, the car to the right gets to go first.

At intersections

If an officer feels you have obstructed the way in an intersection or you have crowded it, he or she can issue a ticket. This is a completely subjective ticket and therefore, you have an excellent chance of beating it when you take it to court.

Failure to yield at uncontrolled or four-way stop

If you hold a driver's license, you should already know that the first person to arrive at a four-way stop gets to proceed first. If you and another driver arrive at the same moment, the driver on the right gets to go first. If you do not follow the correct sequence, you could be issued a ticket.

Often, these particular citations are issued after an accident. Four-way stop signs are not a big concern for police. Characteristically, if two people start to move forward at the same time, they both subsequently step on their brakes and then one driver yields to the other.

If you do get a ticket and fight it, your best line of defense is to prove you entered the intersection first and therefore had the right of way to proceed. You can use diagrams for this presentation, and if you have a witness who was riding with you, it would be extremely helpful for your case if he or she came along to court with you.

Failing to yield at a three-way intersection

The rules are a little different when it comes to three-way stops. The driver who is on the dead-end street must always yield to the other drivers, no matter who got there first. Your main defense to this infraction is identical to the four-way stop — prove you were first to the intersection.

Failure to yield when making a left-hand turn

This is another subjective ticket. Within the language of the law, you are supposed to yield to oncoming traffic when making a left-hand turn, but if the road is open, most drivers take the risk. If an officer determines that your turn was "unsafe," he or she will ticket you. A valid argument in court could be your turn was done with "reasonable safety." Again, a corroborating witness will be the most help, but a diagram illustrating the intersection and the location of traffic in that intersection could also be helpful.

Failure to yield at stop and yield signs

Even if you make a complete stop at a stop sign or red light, you can still receive a ticket if you begin driving before your turn. These citations are normally issued when you approach an intersection with stop signs, then stop, and then proceed through without regard to other cars at the intersection. If there is oncoming traffic, your actions could cause an accident. You must convince the judge that you acted with "reasonable safety."

Challenge the officer's point of view and use diagrams and photographs to mount your defense. If there was a passenger in your car, bring him or her in as a witness to testify you did not put the passenger or anyone else in danger when you crossed the intersection.

Failing to yield to pedestrians

Crosswalks are everywhere. In most states, drivers must yield to pedestrians at a crosswalk. Law enforcement is strict with these tickets because drivers who fail to yield to pedestrians pose a huge risk to the person crossing the street.

If there is no crosswalk and pedestrians are crossing the road, you may have a defense. If you receive a ticket for failing to yield to pedestrians when there is no crosswalk, go back and take photographs. Carefully read the statute you were charged under. In some states, it is written: After a pedestrian crosses in front of your car, you can proceed through the crosswalk, even if the pedestrian is still on the crosswalk. In other cases, the law reads that if you are at an intersection and there is only a marked crosswalk on one side (for example, you are coming from the south side of the intersection and there is only a crosswalk on the north side), the pedestrian must use the marked side; you may proceed ahead of the pedestrian if he or she is using the non-marked side.

Yet, in some states like California, the pedestrian has to be completely off the street before you are allowed to pass through the crosswalk. In situations like this, your only line of defense is to argue that you did wait for the pedestrian and the pedestrian was out of the crosswalk. If you think the officer's line of sight was obstructed, say so — it might mean he or she did not see the entire episode and you have a defense.

Driving Too Slowly

If you want to drive slowly, move over to the right lane, and let everyone who wants to drive the speed limit continue on. Also consider turning on your flashing emergency lights, as this will alert other drivers you are driving at a slowly and steady pace and they should avoid getting too close. Driving too slowly can be dangerous and can cause accidents. If you have been ticketed for driving too slowly, you need to defend your actions.

Possible defenses to this type of moving violation could be the road conditions were simply too dangerous to drive the posted speed limit. This is often the case with severe wind, rain, or snowstorms. Also, if you were in the right lane and a slow tractor was in front of you, it is a viable defense to say you only moved to the left lane while going slow to pass the tractor.

In cases like these, the officer who issued you the citation only has to state that you were driving below the posted speed limit. The burden of proving why you were doing it is entirely on you.

Impeding traffic

Drivers are allowed to impede traffic if the reason they are driving slowly is due to inclement weather conditions. This can also be true if the weather has caused the road to become icy, wet, slick, or littered with branches.

Tailgating

Tailgating is one car closely driving behind another car – this is an aggressive way to drive and can lead to an accident. At least one car length should always be between your car's front bumper and the car in front of you.

The key defense to a beat a tailgating ticket is to prove your distance behind the car in front of you was reasonable and safe, given the road and weather conditions at the time the citation occurred. Generally, on a highway you would need evidence showing that there were between four and eight car lengths between your car and the car in front of you. For city driving, two to four car lengths are the norm. Alternatively, you could present evidence that your tailgating was only the result of a sudden slowdown by the driver in front of you. Testify you did not have time to adjust your speed before the police officer pulled you over.

Statutes are one of the main reasons you will get a ticket if you rear-end someone in an accident. Although the officer did not see the accident, he or she presumes you were following too closely. If you get a tailgating ticket as a result of an accident, you can defend it by stating the other driver stopped suddenly or the other driver made an unsafe lane change and pulled in front of you with too little room to spare. Most tailgating statutes use vague language, like "following too closely than is reasonably safe." You can show your distance was reasonably safe and the other driver is at fault.

When it is time for you to question the officer, be sure to ask whether she can say with complete certainty the accident was a result of your tailgating. It is tough for officers to swear to under oath if they were not at the accident scene when it happened.

Improper Passing

Double painted lines on the road means no passing at all from either direction. Dashed lines on your side of the road means you can legally pass if conditions are safe. Solid lines on your side mean you cannot make a pass, even if conditions are safe. So it should come as no surprise that if you pass where it is not legal, you could get a ticket.

Endangering others

This occurs when you slide over to make a pass and another car is coming straight at you. An officer can give you a ticket if you nearly cause an accident or if the oncoming car has to go off the road to avoid hitting you. The only potential defense here is to show that, in fact, your actions were no danger to others. To make this showing you will need to present evidence of the scene of the incident at the time of the ticket. If you can show the other car was so far away there was no actual danger to it, then you can prevail here. There are, however, a few exceptions to this general rule, as illustrated below.

Blind passing

When you pass a car and cannot see what is coming at you, it constitutes blind passing. It does not matter if you did not put another car in jeopardy or almost cause an accident. Often, you can receive a ticket if you have created the possibility of an accident while attempting to pass in an area where you cannot see what is approaching you. These citations are mostly issued if you pass right before a hill or curve. Since the burden of proof lies with the officer, you can challenge the officer's memory as to your location and how far you were from the hill or curve when you cross-examine him or her in court.

Passing on the right

Passing on the right involves driving around another car from the shoulder of the road, or passing in another unsafe way. If the shoulder of the road is unpaved, it is illegal to go around someone who is turning. Often, you will see a car driving down the road and another driver simply pulling around it on the right because it is going too slowly.

If you are caught doing this, you can challenge whether the shoulder was fully paved. Research the civil engineering definition of a "paved road." Photos will also help in this line of defense.

Criminal Speeding

This is a violation where you should seek the advice of any attorney before fighting it in court. In most states, criminal speeding frequently kicks in when you are driving in gross excess of the posted speed limit. In New Mexico, for example, a person who drives more than 26 miles above the posted speed limit or more than 85 mph, regardless of the posted speed limit, is guilty of a misdemeanor, carrying eight points and fines up to $200. While you can employ the same defenses as you would in any other speeding case, this is an exceedingly serious offense and you need professional assistance, namely the assistance of an attorney.

Seatbelt Violations

All states, but New Hampshire, have some form of laws that make it illegal to drive without wearing your seatbelt. Of these, 30 states have primary seatbelt laws that require anyone sitting in the front seat to be buckled. Nineteen states have secondary laws that only require minors to wear safety belts. A state-by-state list of seatbelt laws can be found at the Governors Highway Safety Association Web site: **www.ghsa.org/html/stateinfo/laws/seatbelt_laws.html**.

With these violations, you may be able to testify in court you had only unbuckled yourself for a second to readjust the belt or you were just getting ready to buckle your seatbelt because you had just pulled out of a parking lot.

Open Container

Open container laws prohibit drivers from having an opened container of alcohol within the passenger compartment of the car. Currently, 43 jurisdictions prohibit any form of open alcohol in the passenger compartment of the car. Arkansas, Connecticut,

Delaware, Mississippi, Missouri, Tennessee, Virginia, and West Virginia allow only passengers to consume alcohol while the car is moving. Mississippi is the lone state that allows a driver to drink while driving, as long as his blood alcohol content level remains below the legal limit. Although these laws are common sense enough, even you may have inadvertently violated them at one time.

Imagine you are at a restaurant, and at the end of the meal your server asks if you want to take home the rest of your bottle of wine — you decide you want to take it home. If you are pulled over for some other violation and the officer notices you or a passenger has a bottle of alcohol that is not properly sealed, he could issue you a citation for violating the open container laws. If he does so, the officer may ask you to take a breathalyzer test to determine blood alcohol content. The highest you can "blow" to pass the test is 0.079 (below 0.08) in all 50 states.

Alternatively, the officer could ask you to undergo a field sobriety test. The Standardized Field Sobriety Test Battery consists of three tests. First, the officer will administer the horizontal gaze nystagmus (HGN) test. This test requires the officer to shine a small flashlight in your eyes. If you cannot follow the light smoothly or your eye jerks when it reaches the edge of your field of vision, this is an indication of intoxication.

The second test is the walk-and-turn. In this test, the driver must take nine steps, heal-to-toe, along a straight line. If the driver does not stay balanced, touch heel to toe, uses his arms to balance, or takes the wrong number of steps, he or she will fail.

Finally, the officer will require the driver to stand on one leg. This test requires the driver to maintain balance for 30 seconds. If the driver loses balance, then he fails this third portion. If you pass the battery of tests, the officer will likely not charge you with driving under the influence; however, you will still be liable for violating the open container law.

Depending on the jurisdiction, there are two potential defenses to an open container violation. In states that do not allow any open containers in the passenger compartment, the only defense you can make is mistake of fact. Open container laws require the driver to knowingly be in the possession of an open container of alcohol. The key here is *knowingly*. If you were unaware that there was an open container in the passenger compartment (for example, unbeknownst to you, a friend brought the alcohol in your car), then you can escape liability. If, however, you were aware of an open container in your car, then you are guilty of the offense.

In jurisdictions that allow passengers to consume while the vehicle is in motion, you can assert that the open container belongs to one of the passengers, and not you. To assert this defense, you will need to show that your passenger was in physical possession of the alcohol. To make this showing, you will likely need to have your friend testify that the bottle belonged to her and also present evidence of the physical location of the bottle: The farther away from you, the better.

CHAPTER 6

Driving Under the Influence

Driving Under the Influence (DUI) is one of the most serious driving offenses. Generally, each individual's first three DUIs are misdemeanor crimes, carrying the possibility of jail time and license suspension. Habitual offenders, however, can face felony prosecution for multiple offenses. As a disclaimer, please seek legal counsel on this type of offense. This chapter will provide information on what certain laws are; this book will not attempt to provide any kind of legal advice on receiving a DUI.

To be charged with a DUI, you do not have to be legally intoxicated to be convicted of this offense. This is why it is called "driving under the influence" instead of drunken driving. You can also be cited for DUI when under the influence of drugs, either prescription or illegal. In all 50 states, the legal "limit" is a blood alcohol content level of 0.08 percent. However, a 6-foot-2-inch man who weighs 200 pounds can consume more drinks than a petite woman who is a foot shorter and 100 pounds lighter. Therefore, it takes more alcohol for a large man to reach 0.08 than it would take a petite woman.

The effects of alcohol reach your brain within seconds of ingestion it. As a result, you have less effective vision and hearing, experience clumsiness and lack of muscular coordination, and you have a lack of judgment and self-control, which is a direct result of the euphoric feeling you get from drinking. While the 0.08 percent seems to be a relative number when it comes to determining if an individual is driving under the influence, it is not. In the late 1930s, the American Medical Association (AMA) held a "Committee to Study Problems of Motor Vehicle Accidents." The committee researched blood alcohol levels to determine at what percentage an individual is actually "under the influence" and unable to operate a motor vehicle. As a result of this study, the AMA and the National Safety Council concluded several things:

- At a blood alcohol content level of 0.05 percent or less, no persons were under the influence of alcohol.

- At a blood alcohol content level between 0.05 and 0.15 percent, a person may or may not be under the influence, depending on any number of circumstances. These circumstances included height, weight, whether they had eaten, how fast they drank, or if they were on any prescription medications.

- At a blood alcohol content level above the 0.15 percent mark, a person was absolutely intoxicated and under the influence. These people were completely impaired and not able to drive a motor vehicle.

To be charged with a DUI, your blood alcohol content level does not have to be 0.08 percent or higher. A person with a blood alcohol content of 0.08 or higher is per se intoxicated. Some states, however, do not rely exclusively on this limit. These jurisdictions will still find a driver guilty of DUI, even if he or she registered below that level, if the prosecution can otherwise prove he was impaired. To do this, the prosecution will have to provide corroborating evidence. This could include failure of a field sobriety test and erratic driving prior to being pulled over. You would still receive a ticket, but it would be a non-waivable offense. In essence, the officer would likely take you to jail until you sobered up. You would have to show up for court.

Driving under the influence is a complicated area of the law, therefore, seek legal advice before trying to fight the ticket. Almost every town has a lawyer who specializes in DUIs. These attorneys generally charge a flat fee for each offense. In selecting an attorney, you should look for two qualities. First, make sure the attorney has taken at least some offenses to trial. This is necessary because DUIs rely on scientific tests to determine blood alcohol content. Your attorney should be skilled at questioning the validity of the tests administered. Second, look for an attorney who has a long track record of favorable settlements. If your blood alcohol content was over 0.08 percent, beating the ticket is going to be difficult. In these cases, an attorney who has a long-standing relationship with the prosecutor's office is going to give you the best shot at negotiating a favorable plea.

The rest of this chapter will go over what to expect in terms of insurance and the types of fines and suspensions you may be facing.

What you Were Charged With

To face a conviction for driving under the influence, the state has the burden of proving you were in actual physical control of a vehicle, and while you were in physical control of the vehicle, you were under the influence of an intoxicating liquor or drug, or you have a blood alcohol content of 0.08 within two hours of when you were operating a vehicle.

While you do not have much of a chance to dispute the element of actually operating the vehicle, you do have the opportunity to dispute whether you were intoxicated while operating it. In other words, if you had an alcoholic drink and then got in your car and started driving, you may get pulled over for speeding before your system has even had a chance to recognize the alcoholic beverage. However, if your blood alcohol content test is taken a little later, your body will have begun metabolizing that drink and your reading will be much higher than when you initially had the drink. Although, most statutes consider a person intoxicated if they have a blood alcohol content of 0.08 or greater within two hours after driving, so an officer can still issue a citation even if you were not above the limit at the time you were driving.

It is important for you to understand there is a delay in time between when you actually have an alcoholic drink and when your body metabolizes that drink. It is similar to when you are eating dinner; just because you have already put food in your mouth, you still feel hungry because your brain has not recognized there is food in your stomach. Once you stop drinking, your blood alcohol level will decrease as time passes. Blood alcohol content levels drop at a rate of roughly 0.02 percent per hour. This can work either in your favor or against you. The prosecution may say that if your reading was at a 0.07 percent when the officer took your reading, it was at a 0.09 percent when you got in your car and started operating it the hour before.

Now, take a look at the tests that can be used to determine your blood alcohol content. There are three tests in most states — the breath test, the urine test, and the blood test. All three are designed to determine the actual alcohol content in your body.

Understanding the Tests

Typically, when you are pulled over because an officer suspects you are driving under the influence, you will first be asked to take a *field sobriety test*. It is important you know these tests are entirely voluntary in each state and there is no penalty if you refuse to take them.

Field sobriety tests

These tests were developed by different police agencies to help police officers make roadside determinations as to whether a driver is under the influence of alcohol or drugs. Tests such as the "alphabet test" or the "toe-to-toe" test are both considered field sobriety tests, nonetheless, the only three field sobriety tests that are sanctioned by the National Highway Traffic and Safety Administration (NHTSA: **www.nhtsa.dot.gov**) are the "walk and turn" test, "one leg" test, and "horizontal gaze nystagmus" (involuntary eye movement) test.

Your performance on these tests determines whether the officer will give you a breathalyzer test. It may also give him probable cause to arrest you.

Defense attorneys have been known to criticize the accuracy of field sobriety tests. Many defense attorneys have been quoted as saying they are "designed to fail." In response, the NHTSA states that if the three tests they sanction are not administered correctly or if they are conducted in a manner that does not adhere to the training protocols, the validity of the tests could be "compromised." *Field sobriety tests have already been discussed at length in Chapter 6.*

Aside from the field sobriety tests, there are other methods to determine whether you are driving under the influence.

The blood test

Many times, your blood will not be drawn until you get to the police station.

A blood test administrator will take a sample of your blood and measure the amount of alcohol in it. Due to the way this test is administered, only a qualified person may draw your blood. Who is technically "qualified" to draw your blood varies from state to state. Most states, however, allow either the police or hospital personnel to draw blood — the choice is yours. If you elect to have the police draw blood, they will ask you to sign a waiver of liability.

Furthermore, because blood tests qualify as both scientific and physical evidence, the state must adhere to certain procedures to ensure the veracity and reliability of the test. For scientific evidence to be admissible in a court, the prosecution will have to call an expert to interpret the results and testify to their reliability. Any driver challenging the veracity of their results will also need her own expert witness. Furthermore, because this is physical evidence, the prosecution will also have the burden of establishing the chain of evidence. In essence, this means they will need to account for the whereabouts of the blood from the moment it left your arm until the test results were obtained. To do this, the state will have to elicit a testimony that the police officer drew your blood, labeled it, and transported it to the lab for testing.

While blood tests are usually accurate, if an unqualified person administers the test, the results could be inaccurate. One typical error is testing just the blood serum instead of the whole blood. A test of the blood serum tends to skew the results toward a higher blood alcohol content. If this was the case, the results of a blood test could be called in to question in a court of law. View information on this at ExpertLaw.com's Web site at **www.expertlaw. com**. Under "Popular Law Articles," click on the link that reads

"Drunk Driving." This will take you to articles on "Blood Alcohol Testing in Drunk Driving Cases."

The breath test

Also relatively accurate, this is the one most commonly administered on the side of the road. A police officer will ask you to blow into the breathalyzer. If a driver fails a field sobriety test, the officer usually asks the driver to take the breath test.

If you have consumed a reasonable number of drinks relative to your body weight, your blood alcohol content level will probably be low. If this is the case, an officer may decide to not cite you for a DUI. However, remember that a long, deep breath will contain more alcohol and result in a higher concentration of alcohol on the breath test. The officer may instruct you to breathe this way to get the most accurate results.

The urine test

The final test that can determine your blood alcohol content level is the urine test. This test is the most inaccurate and therefore, is open to more questions and disputes in the courtroom. In many states, the urine test can only be submitted as evidence if the blood and breath tests results are both unavailable. Since the urine test has to be equivalent to a blood alcohol content level, it can give a misleading reading. For example, if you were to have four drinks, but stop two hours before driving, because of the time it takes for your body to metabolize alcohol your urine could show a higher reading than your actual blood level at the time you are driving. Conversely, if you were to drink four beers very quickly just moments before driving and taking a urine test, the delay in metabolizing would result in a level that is below the actual blood alcohol content. Consequently, this can work both for and against you in court. On one hand, the prosecution could argue the test was too low and you were actually more intoxicated than reflected by the urine test. On the other hand, you could argue that you were actually coming down from being more intoxicated. The farther in time you last consumed, the better your chances of prevailing on this argument.

How Alcohol Interacts with Your Body

Each person metabolizes alcohol differently, depending on height, weight, gender, metabolic rate, and other factors. However, the actual function of metabolizing alcohol is the same. Alcohol depresses your central nervous system at an increasing rate as alcohol is absorbed into the blood stream. First the alcohol is absorbed, then distributed, and finally eliminated.

What your body does with alcohol

When you consume alcohol, it undergoes a unique process. Unlike food, which takes hours to digest, your stomach absorbs alcohol directly into your bloodstream. What your stomach does not catch is quickly absorbed by your small intestine. Over the course of an hour, your blood alcohol level will continue to rise, even if you have stopped consuming.

When you consume alcohol, it goes into your bloodstream, which sends it to your body tissue. Your veins continue to let the alcohol flow in your bloodstream, and carry it also to your lungs where the blood becomes oxygenated. Arteries then carry the oxygen-rich blood to the brain and the rest of the body. Alcohol is water-soluble, so the alcohol content in the whole body is directly proportional to your total body water content. Each person is built differently in regard to gender, weight, height, body fat, and tolerance; therefore, water content varies in each person.

This means that the more water there is in your body, the more alcohol it takes to affect you. People with more muscle mass have more water in their bodies than those with more body fat because body fat has little water and thus cannot absorb much alcohol. Women naturally have a higher body fat percentage than men, so they will be more affected by the same amount of alcohol. On average, a woman's body is 55 percent water weight, while a man's is about 68 percent.

An adult can metabolize about one drink each hour. One standard-sized drink is defined as:

- One 1.5-oz. shot of 100-proof liquor or distilled spirits.

- One 5-oz. glass of wine.

- One regular 12-oz. beer (about 6 percent alcohol by volume).

- Remember that microbrewery beer, malt liquor, pint bottles of beer, large wine glasses, 20 percent alcohol wines, and extremely strong or large mixed drinks should be counted differently.

If you are at the bar and drinking 12-oz. glasses of regular beer, it will take you about an hour to metabolize each one. Some say that they are fine to drive as long as they only have one drink an hour, depending on gender and body weight. For example, they may or may not be right. For the average person, 60 percent of the alcohol he has consumed will be absorbed in to his bloodstream within a half-hour. About 90 percent will be absorbed into his bloodstream within one hour, and the alcohol will be completely absorbed within an hour and a half. Within an hour of your first drink, though, your body will start to process and eliminate the alcohol.

Additionally, several other factors affect how quickly your body is able to get rid of alcohol:

- Healthy people have the ability to process alcohol more efficiently than unhealthy people.

- Chronic alcoholics whose livers function properly metabolize alcohol more quickly than the average person.

- People in their 20s, for example, metabolize alcohol more efficiently than people who are older, for example, people in their 40s.

Calculating Approximate Blood Alcohol Levels

If you are reading this book for help with another, non-alcohol-related traffic ticket, this section may be useful to you. There is a simple formula to calculate your approximate blood alcohol level. This should not be a steadfast rule to determine how much you can or cannot drink and still be under the legal limit. However, you should not drive at all after consuming even one drink. This calculation can show you how long it takes to metabolize alcohol — consider driving only after your body is completely finished metabolizing.

- Take the number 3.8 and divide it by your body weight.

- You should get a number between 0.015 and 0.040.

- This number is the maximum percentage of alcohol that will be added to your bloodstream per drink.

- After 40 minutes from the time you started drinking, your body begins to eliminate alcohol at a rate of 0.01 percent per 40 minutes you were drinking.

- Multiply the number of drinks that you have consumed by the number you calculated between 0.015 and 0.040. Subtract 0.01 for every 40 minutes that you have been drinking. Do not count the first 40 minutes.

- The result is your approximate blood alcohol level.

For example, a woman who consumes three drinks over the course of two hours, or 120 minutes, would have an equation such as:

- 3.8 divided by 140 pounds = 0.027 percent.

- Three drinks multiplied by 0.027 percent = 0.081.

- The woman has been drinking for 120 minutes, and she would subtract 0.02 from 0.081. (Do not count the first 40 minutes).

Her approximate blood alcohol level would be 0.061 percent after drinking three regular drinks within 120 minutes.

The breathalyzer test works by measuring alcohol that is evaporated from the bloodstream into the lungs. Since the bottom of your lungs is nearest to the bloodstream, the air in that area has the highest concentration of alcohol. For this reason, an officer will ask a suspected driver to make a long, full exhale into the machine. An adult body can eliminate alcohol at a rate of 0.15 blood alcohol concentration per hour and, because of this low rate of elimination, a person who has consumed a substantial amount of alcohol can wake up after a long night's sleep still feeling its effects. Furthermore, an empty stomach absorbs alcohol more quickly than a full one.

Police officers administer breathalyzer tests at the time he or she arrests the driver, and another an hour later when the driver has been sitting at the station. If the readings are close, officers know you could be solidly charged. If there is a drastic drop in the second reading, the police need to consider that there were other factors involved in your initial reading.

While police do not ask you if you have had anything to eat or if you know what your percentage of body fat is while they have you on the side of the road, these are all issues to address with your attorney. The state will not raise these issues in court because it could cast a shadow of doubt on the evidence that they have to convict you. Though, done right, an attorney may be able to enter these into evidence and help sway the court's decision.

Offenses and Penalties for Drunk Driving

Under 21

In all states, 21 is the legal age to drink alcohol. If you are driving while intoxicated before then, your license will be taken and you will face a host of other misdemeanor charges such as "Minor in Possession of Alcohol." This applies whether you test at the legal limit of 0.08 or not. Those under the age 21 are under the "zero tolerance rule."

21 or older and first offense

Many states now require a minimum of one to seven days in jail and up to a maximum of six months for a first offense DUI. Additionally, fines start at $500 plus court cost for first-time offenders.

21 or older and second offense

A second DUI will result in more jail time and higher fines. In Illinois, for example, a second offense carries a $1,500 fine, up to one year in jail, a one-year suspension of your driver's license, and community service. California requires 48 hours in jail, and fines up to $1,400. Because laws vary by state, you should consult your state's statutes.

21 or older and third or subsequent offense

You will still suffer all the same penalties as your second offense. However, fines will be in excess of $2,500 on average, plus court costs. Additionally, some states have habitual offender statutes for drivers with three or more DUIs with a certain period of time. Tennessee, for example, defines a habitual offender as one who committed three DUIs within five years. Habitual offenders could be prosecuted as felons and lose their licenses for up to ten years.

Felony DUI

If you are involved in a motor vehicle accident while you are intoxicated and someone is either injured or killed, you will face a felony charge. In New York, for example, vehicular manslaughter is a Class D felony, which includes a prison term not to exceed five years and a fine up to $7,500. Due to the intensity of the offense, you should never fight a felony charge on your own. Seek the counsel of an attorney who has experience in this offense.

License suspension penalties

In the past, driver's licenses were not necessarily suspended for their first DUI charge. Over time, as previously mentioned, the public's attitude toward drunken driving has changed. As a result, laws and penalties have become harsher. Almost all 50 states now suspend your driver's license before any drunken driving conviction, whether it is your first or your third. The state's Department of Motor Vehicle (DMV) Office will suspend the license. In many states, your suspension is handed to you by the police officer who issues the ticket, however, you can typically apply for a hardship license. To be eligible for this license you will need to show why you need to be able to drive during the suspension period. Reasons for this include doctor's visits, to get to work, driving to church, or to transport children to school.

After issuing you a citation, the arresting officer will then fill out and send the necessary paperwork to the DMV. This paperwork documents all the facts at the time of the stop and also any important notes the officer thinks are significant enough to aid in your possible conviction in court. These are referred to as "sworn statements," "police reports," "evidence," or "discovery."

When the DMV receives these documents from the officer who arrested you for DUI, the DMV officials review them. If all the information is found to be in order by the DMV clerk, then a driver's license suspension will be imposed 30 days after your arrest. This suspension happens before, and in addition to, any suspension the court may hand down at the time of your trial. The suspension will start on the 31st day after your arrest, unless you demand a DMV Administrative Hearing; the time line to do so varies by state, so be sure to call your local office and ask how long you have to file the paperwork. The length of the suspension depends on many possible factors that may exist in your case.

How to Deal with a DUI Charge

You should never deal with a DUI charge on your own. Cases like these are best left to a professional attorney. In most courtrooms, a judge will be hesitant to let you represent yourself. Since you stand to lose so much from a drunken driving conviction, the legal system wants to know you have been properly represented.

What if I cannot afford an attorney?

If you cannot afford an attorney and you are facing time in jail, it is your constitutional right to be screened for a court-appointed attorney at the expense of the state. The income guidelines vary from state to state. To find out if you qualify, contact your local public defender's office and ask for an application and a copy of their income guidelines.

How your trial will play out

There are several things to consider when you are released from jail after being arrested for driving under the influence. One of them is how to proceed with your case. If you immediately leave jail and head to an attorney's office, the attorney will likely go over the procedures with you. If you cannot afford a large retainer (Between $500 to $2,500, depending on how many prior offenses you have) for an attorney, you will head to the courthouse on arraignment day with no representation except for yourself. Arraignment is the processes where you will appear before a magistrate judge and enter a plea of guilty or not guilty.

Most states will allow you a trial-by-jury, although the U.S. Supreme Court has ruled differently in the past. As a general rule, if the offense is a felony or punishable by more than six months in jail, you are constitutionally entitled to a jury trial. You will need to file a motion for a jury trial if you want your case heard before a jury of your peers. This is called a "Jury Trial Request" (JTR). There are a few exceptions to this rule. If you reside in Hawaii, Louisiana, or Nevada, you are not entitled to a jury trial. If you live in Alaska, New Hampshire, or Virginia, you are entitled to a jury trial only on appeal after a bench trial with only a judge. Acquittals in drunken driving case are low. California, for example, boasts a 79 percent convictions rate. Consequently, be wary of an overly optimistic attorney. Unless there is an obvious mistake in the testing or your arrest was unconstitutional, you might not win your case.

What Do I Stand to Lose with a Drunken Driving Conviction?

There are many things you stand to lose under a drunken driving conviction on your record. Your job could be at stake, your insurance rates will go up, your insurance carrier may even drop your coverage, and you may not be able to travel outside the country.

Loss of job

If you have a drunken driving conviction on your record, some employers may not want to hire you. This is especially true if you apply for a job, which requires driving a company vehicle on either a regular basis or even just once per year. If you hold a professional license such as a pilot, doctor, or lawyer's, you could lose it as a result of your driving under the influence charge. Every state differs on how many years a driving record goes back. For some states, the record is only tracked back three years, while others go back ten years. Your driving history could be checked when you sign pre-employment paperwork.

If you are currently employed, discuss how to approach your employer with your attorney. Depending on the policies of the company you work for, you may not be obligated to disclose the violation to your employer until after the trial and potential conviction.

However, if you are employed by a federal agency, your DUI stop will most likely be brought to their attention long before your assigned court date.

Another aspect to consider is the amount of time you will miss from work if you serve jail time due to a DUI conviction. If it is seven days and you have accrued paid vacation time, you may be able to use that and not ever tell your employer. However, if you must be in jail for several months, you are not likely to get that much time off, even if you take it as unpaid leave.

Car insurance

Dealing with your car insurance company after a DUI can be aggravating. Even if DUI charges are dropped your car insurance may go up. The arrest itself creates paperwork that states you were under the influence while driving.

If you requested a hearing following the DUI arrest and you win at the hearing, your driver's license suspension will be set aside. If you are unsuccessful at the hearing, then the suspension will be imposed sometime after the hearing. Remember, you are still not out of the woods with the court. When this happens, you will have what is referred to as an "administrative suspension" on your driving record — a red flag with your insurance company. On top of the "administrative suspension," if you end up being convicted of driving under the influence, the court will update the DMV's records; this means that the conviction will show up on your driving record.

Keep in mind, while an insurance company usually checks your driving record when your policy is renewed, they might do random checks as well. When you are arrested for driving under the influence, most states require you to file a mandatory SR-22. This is a form that must be completed by your insurance company, per the rules of the DMV. This tells your insurance company that your driving record should be checked.

Every state except for New Hampshire and Wisconsin require that drivers carry car insurance. An SR-22 is much like bankruptcy because it follows you around for years and flags the applicable company that you are a high-risk individual. An SR-22 does not stay with you forever, just like a bankruptcy; in most cases, an SR-22 is only required for the first three years after the DUI arrest.

However, if you fail to file the required SR-22 every time you renew your car insurance or if there is any lapse in your coverage after you reinstate your license, the DMV will suspend your driving privileges again.

Once your insurance company learns of the DUI charge, they are likely to take some form of action. This action will largely depend on your past driving record and what insurance company you have. If you already have many moving violation tickets on your driving record, chances are they will either drop you entirely or raise your premium. If you have not had a ticket in the last ten years and then you are convicted for drunken driving, the company may raise your rates, but not drop you. Some car insurance companies are incredibly strict about the amount of risk they will allow, especially after such a serious charge. Even if it is your first traffic infraction and you have been with the same insurance company for a long time, you may still be dropped after your policy expires.

Traveling rights

Many countries classify any "crime" as a reason to refuse or limit entry in to the country.

Since over 96 percent of DUI convictions are classified as misdemeanors, your DUI will be listed on a criminal record. (The other 4 percent are classified as felonies.) This means the chances are slim you will be able to travel out of the country after being tagged with a DUI. To find out if the country you are traveling to has limitations for admission based on criminal convictions, check with the consular for the country to which you want to travel.

Military admission

A DUI charge on your record must be cleared up before joining the military. To do this, you need to try to get the DUI expunged from your record. Not only is this an embarrassing incident, it takes a lot of time and effort on both your part, the court's part, and the part of the recruiting office that is trying to sign you up. To get an expungement, file suit with the state. Generally, you must wait a certain period of time after the conviction, and you must have not committed subsequent offenses. Currently, only seven states offer expungement procedures for DUIs: California, Utah, Nevada, Florida, New York, Washington, and Texas.

CHAPTER 7

Do You Need a Lawyer?

While this book is about fighting your traffic ticket without a licensed attorney, there are times when you should not fight your case alone: DUIs and reckless driving offenses, for example. Therefore, you should know the facts about hiring an attorney for your case. You may wonder, "Why would I pay a lawyer hundreds of dollars an hour to defend a $300 traffic ticket?" There are times when you should retain a lawyer, no doubt. For example, if you stand to lose your license or face spending any time in jail, you want an attorney. One of the best ways to determine if you should seek legal counsel is to ask yourself two simple questions: what can I lose, and can I afford to lose it? If the answers to your questions are "A lot," and "No, I cannot," chances are you should seek the assistance of a professional attorney.

This chapter will include how to determine if you need an attorney, what you should look for and expect in your legal counsel, the types of attorneys that are available, and what they can and cannot do for you.

Types of Attorneys

As with every other profession, attorneys specialize in different areas of the law. Relatively few attorneys specialize in minor traffic infractions. There are many more who specialize in defending those who stand accused of driving under the influence of drugs or alcohol.

Private attorneys

These are attorneys who practice law in small offices either alone or with one or two other lawyers. You should call several of these offices and make an appointment with at least one if possible. Most law firms will offer a free initial consultation. You should take advantage of this meeting to find out how likely you are to prevail and if the attorney charges a flat fee or by the hour. Attorneys who offer free consultations will often advertise it in their advertisements. Also, many private attorneys are focused on areas such as criminal law, family law, and real estate law, so make sure you find an attorney who has experience in the offense under which you are charged.

Group legal services and prepaid legal services

Many employers offer employees the option of buying in to group legal services or into a prepaid legal service plan. In the event the employee needs an attorney, they can draw from the group pool of attorneys the employer is contracted with.

Again, you will have similar circumstances as with the sector of private practice attorneys. Some group legal services are excellent and others are mediocre. Either way, you need to be sure the attorney is versed in traffic court. Ask the attorney how many cases she has tried and how long she has been in practice. You are normally guaranteed a free consultation with group legal services and prepaid legal services because they have contracted with your employer in some way.

Public defenders

When facing more serious traffic charges that involve jail time (including a DUI or criminal speeding), you need an attorney. It is your Constitutional right for the court to appoint an attorney if you cannot afford to hire one and this appointment will be done at the expense of the state.

However, public defenders do have limitations. For one, income guidelines vary in each state. In most states, you need to be below the Federal poverty line to be considered eligible for a free attorney. If you are only facing a minor traffic charge, you will not be eligible for this service at all.

Furthermore, in some states there is a cap on what the court-appointed attorney may charge the court. Some individuals believe this cap keeps the attorney from working his or her hardest on the case. In some states, public defenders are paid a yearly salary regardless of how many hours they put in or cases they win.

Three Ways an Attorney Can Help You

What if you are one of the millions of drivers who have received a traffic ticket but are not facing an astronomical fine? You are still a little nervous about handling it alone, yet you truly cannot justify spending a lot of money on an attorney to do something you are able to do on your own. Understand that you can still consult an attorney, and likely at a reduced cost. If an attorney believes you are considering hiring him or her, it is possible to receive a free consultation that lasts a half an hour or a full hour. During the consultation, you can ask the attorney questions and get a feel for what kind of chance you have, and what line of defense he or she would likely use.

An office consultation

This involves calling a number of attorneys and making an appointment to speak with one or more of them. Your consultation will either be free of charge or you will incur a minimal fee, likely less than $100. While you will not have representation during the trial, you may be able to get a few of your questions answered, a better grasp on your legal position, and the pros and cons of your options spelled out in an understandable manner for you. This is a service that you must shop around for — some attorneys will give you a full consultation and some will not. Some may require a retainer (a down payment, essentially) before getting in to too much detail about what defensive legal strategy they would take. Also, not all attorneys are equipped to handle DUI charges.

Negotiation

When you are facing more serious traffic charges such as a DUI, or you stand to lose your license because of an excessive number of traffic tickets you have received, you need the negotiation skills of an attorney.

Not only that, their relationships with the prosecutors and judges could play in your favor. These relationships can exist in honest ways and can be the difference between you winning and losing your case.

This may not be true if you are facing the more serious DUI charges.

Representing you in court

If you are faced with the more serious charges — including drunken driving, criminal speeding, and reckless driving — and there is no chance of negotiation, you will need to be represented in court by a licensed attorney. Not only will an attorney be able to mount a more effective defense than you could as an inexperienced pro-se defendant, he or she also knows far more than you about pre-trial tactics. These mistakes are not as debilitating in trials for simpler infractions like running a traffic light, but in larger cases, these mistakes are important.

- Being disorganized

- Not focusing the court's attention on the most crucial details

These are two mistakes you cannot afford to make when you are facing jail time or the loss of your license.

What An Attorney Can and Cannot Do For You

Depending on the severity of your charges, an attorney can only do so much for your case. The less severe the charge (such as failure to stop, five to ten miles over the speed limit, and lane change violations), the more they will be able to do for you, at a reasonable rate. While attorneys may not be able to do much when it comes to a more severe charge, their personal relationships may make the process go more smoothly.

When do you absolutely need an attorney?

You will need an attorney when:

- You are facing a felony traffic charge, like vehicular homicide.

- You have been charged with driving under the influence of drugs or alcohol.

- You stand to lose your license or become a habitual offender (you have had more than three offenses in a three- to five-year period).

- The impending traffic ticket could mean the difference between keeping your job and losing it (if your job requires you to be able to drive).

How to get the most for your money

Opinions vary as to whether judges prefer defendants who are well versed in their defense. However, it is in your best interest to know what is going on in your case and to pay attention to what your attorney is doing.

For starters, be involved in your defense. If you have read this far in the book, you know about the traffic laws and how to do your own legal research. If you skipped over those chapters, go back and read them. Knowing how to navigate legal research can be an invaluable tool in staying involved in your traffic case.

Your attorney, should you chose to hire one, should be:

- Responsive to you and the needs of your case.

- Your attorney should never be late to a meeting, whether it is in his or her office or another venue. Your attorney should give you a courtesy call to notify you of potential tardiness.

- Your attorney should not schedule a meeting with you within several hours of being in court for another case. Court schedules are unpredictable and can often be off by several hours. Your attorney runs the risk of having to call you last minute to cancel the appointment.

- If you have questions, your attorney should explain answers in a logical way that makes you comfortable.

- An attorney should disclose whether he is capable of handling a more complex charge. He can either refuse to represent you because he does not have experience in the area, or he can offer to learn more about it. An attorney is not required to disclose the information; he can just refuse to represent you.

- Your attorney should address your concerns and fully understand them. She should also fully understand what you hope to get out of the case and her representation.

- For every letter that is sent, motion that is filed, or brief that is written, you should get a copy for your file. Review these mailings and be sure that you agree with what your attorney is doing and the course of action she is taking. Also, be sure that she is only sending necessary documents — this is to ensure your attorney does not bill you for unnecessary work.

- If possible, try to pay your lawyer based on the work he produces, rather than an upfront retainer. You most likely will not be able to avoid the retainer altogether. After the initial retainer is gone, you may be able to work out a different payment plan. Paying as you go allows you the freedom to sever ties at any time without worrying about getting your money back, and it also serves as incentive to your attorney to keep him working on your case.

CHAPTER 8

Proceeding Without an Attorney (Pro Se)

When and Why You Can Do it Yourself

For minor traffic infractions that do not have a penalty involving jail, the loss of your license, the possibility of losing your job, or infractions that are considered felonies, you can and should fight your traffic ticket pro-se. An attorney will charge you upward of $100 per hour to fight a $200 traffic ticket. You may be tempted to just pay it and move on, but consider the other options. Paying a traffic ticket can have many consequences. These include fines, increased insurance rates, and in some cases, license suspensions. The end result of a traffic conviction is motivation enough to do your research, prepare for a trial, and mount your defense.

Play the part

- Dress the part: Wear appropriate clothes when you go to court. This will let the judge know that you respect the process and can be taken seriously.

- Know what to expect: A working knowledge of the way the court system operates will assist in your endeavor. Your best sources of information when it comes to the court and the proceedings will be those who work at the courthouse. For example, the clerk of the court can be a wealth of information about when to file and where to file it. Do not be shy or too prideful to ask questions when you need help. There are so many details to be handled in court matters that just one little bit of wrong information can put your rights in traffic court at jeopardy.

Take a tour

Walk through the halls of the building and get a feel for the environment. Observe trials in progress to get a feeling for how public defenders, prosecutors, judges, and jurors do their jobs; the customs and traditions of the court procedures; and the formalities of the proceedings. This exercise will also alleviate much of the anxiety that you will feel leading up to your trial date. Take some time to find out when traffic court is held. Sit in traffic court if you can and watch for the following. Court cases are public events, so you will not need special permission to observe.

- How the attorneys address the judge.

- The order of events.

- How the hearing is conducted.

- Who starts the arguments.

- How much argument the court allows.

- What limitations appear to be imposed on both sides (for example, whether you can approach witnesses while they are on the stand, how many copies of documents you need to present to the court, and time limitations on examination of witnesses and arguments).

Your presence in the courtroom, particularly if it is filled with jurors, is essential to your case. You want to be taken seriously, even if you proceed pro se. Here are some things to remember while you are representing yourself:

- Always be courteous

- Stand up when you are introduced to the judge and/ or jury

- Always stand when you address the court — no exceptions

- When responding to anything the judge says to you, always say, "Yes, your Honor"

- Always be respectful toward the judge, bailiffs, court reporter, and prosecutor

- Wait your turn to speak; do not interrupt

- Be professional, neat, and organized

Given all the different divisions of the court system, traffic court is the division that the largest numbers of people are familiar with. Every minor traffic infraction, contested summons, license or registration infraction, and other traffic or automobile violation passes through its doors. In a way, that is a good thing, because the end result of seeing so many cases is the atmosphere often becomes much more relaxed and the rules lean on the informal side.

Acting pro se in traffic court can be beneficial for a number of reasons. If the officer who issued the summons does not show up for your trial or cannot remember the conditions on the day you were ticketed, your case will be dismissed.

As previously discussed, by doing your legal research and studying the rule book and statutes, you may find a mistake, loophole, or piece of information that will give you a chance to win your case. Remember, if you plan to act pro se in traffic court, you still must know information about your traffic violation.

Verify your court date

Call the courthouse before the date on your ticket to find out exactly what needs to be done to fight your citation. If you cannot speak to the person you need on the phone, personally go to the courthouse and speak with a clerk.

As an alternative option, many courthouses have Web sites with this information. Some only have the hours of operation and address, while other sites have detailed sections with frequently asked questions that detail how traffic violations are handled in that jurisdiction. Still, others even have online systems to pay your traffic fine, which makes it incredibly easy to plead guilty and move on.

If you do manage to speak directly with a clerk, have your traffic ticket with you and find out the following information:

- Whether the date on your ticket indicates your actual court date, or if that date is just the deadline by which you must contest your ticket.

- Ask if it is possible to have an extension granted so you can truly decide if you want to contest the ticket and schedule a trial date.

- In place of a court hearing, ask if you are eligible for traffic school.

Deciding How to Plead

With this basic information, it is time to decide what course of action you are going to take. You have four basic choices:

- Pay the fine and attend traffic school (if it is an option)

- Plead guilty with an explanation

- Plead *nolo contendere*

- Plead not guilty

Pay the fine

Before you decide to pay the fine, remember it will show up on your driving record and remain there for about a period of three years. While this single violation may not hurt you now, you never know when you will be faced with another traffic ticket. You may not be able to fight the next one. If, on the other hand, you are set in your determination to give up your money without a fight, most courts will allow you to pay your ticket by mail. Some jurisdictions even allow you to pay online. It is a rare instance when you will have to go to court and admit your guilt before writing your check. These instances often arise when you have been charged with an alcohol-related offense or excessive speeding.

Guilty

In this case, you most likely did what the ticket says, but you feel you have a reasonable explanation for your actions. For example, "I made the illegal lane change to avoid being hit by the bales of hay that were falling off a truck." While you will still plead guilty to the judge, your explanation for your actions may help to per-suade the judge to give you a reduced fine or suspend the fine altogether. The offense will still appear on your driving record and your insurance rates may rise, but you may end up with a reduced fine.

Nolo contendere

A plea of *nolo contendere* means you choose not to contest the charge. This is the plea that makes sense if you have been in an accident and received a ticket for it. A *nolo contendere* plea admits to the court that you are not disputing the facts presented. However, it allows for your admission of guilt to not be used in other cases, such as a civil case for damages to the car you hit.

On the other hand, if you were to plead guilty to this, your guilty plea could be used against you in the civil trial. If you believe that you may face a civil lawsuit stemming from your traffic ticket, this can be a option that is critical for you to explore.

Not guilty

You can almost always do this by mail or telephone (this will be the number of the clerk's office for the court, in your local phone book), or by using a traffic court kiosk at the courthouse. If none of these options are available to you, find the courthouse location, go to it, and ask a counter clerk how to plead not guilty. While you are at the clerk's window, ask for a continuance. A continuance is simply a request to push back your hearing date to a more convenient time. There are many reasons you may want to delay your trial. For example, you may need more time to prepare for trial or you may be out of town on the date the trial is scheduled.

A request to delay a trial must be made in writing at least one week before the trial — more if possible. Send copies of the request to both the prosecutor's office and the police department where the officer is employed. Most continuances that are requested in advance of a trial are granted, while those that are requested on the day of the trial are often denied. If granted, the original hearing date will be dismissed and a new hearing date will be set. Many courts hear their traffic cases for specific departments on specific days. Officers know this and will plan their vacations around it.

Conversely, if you request a continuance, the court will often give you a court date wherever it may fit on the calendar, which is not necessarily in line with the normal hearing schedule. This new trial date my fall within a day off for the officer, and you also have the advantage that his or her mind may be less clear about the details after a significant delay in the proceedings. By pleading not guilty, you have a chance that the officer will not be able to show up in court on the date and time the hearing is scheduled. If the officer does not show up for court, your case is dismissed, relieving you from any obligation to pay a fine or receiving points from the ticket on your driving record.

Things to Keep in Mind About a Continuance

If your request for a continuance was not granted, you have a few options. Show the judge proof that a request was mailed and that you have legitimate reasons for requesting a continuance. If that does not work, you can proceed with the trial and try to mount a defense as best as possible with the evidence you have available. There are times when the scheduled trial date conflicts with the officer's or prosecutor's scheduled vacation. If this is the case, they are required to notify you, by mail, of the change in court date. If the court does not have enough time to notify you by mail, they must call you on the phone.

The day before the trial, preferably late in the day, call the clerk's office to see if the continuance has been granted for the prosecution. If it has not, show up in court at your scheduled date and time. When it is your turn to be heard and the prosecution argues that they are not ready, you can argue that you object to the delay because you have taken off time from work to be available for trial at this specific time. It may work in your favor.

If it does not, and it appears the court will still grant the continuance request for the prosecution, check on the "speedy trial" rules for your state and find out if they apply to traffic court. Speedy trial rules set forth how long after the time you are charged with an offense that you must have a trial. For example, for traffic court, state laws might state that you are entitled to a trial within three months of being issued a ticket. It is important to note, however, that speedy trial rules have an exception if the delay in getting to trial was a result of your actions. So, if you file a continuance, be wary that you could be extending the speedy trial period to however long the continuance period was for. If there was a speedy trial violation, however, bring this up at your new trial date and ask that the case be dismissed on the grounds that the trial as scheduled will violate the speedy trial rules.

What if I need an interpreter?

In a court of law, you must be provided with an interpreter if you feel that your English is not strong enough to conduct a trial on your own.

This does not mean that you need to hire an attorney, but you do need to let the court know that you would like the services of an interpreter. In some states, they will not provide an interpreter free of charge for a traffic hearing. The clerk of the court will be able to tell you if this is a free service the court provides. If the court does not provide a free interpreter, enlist one. An interpreter must be a third party who is not involved or biased in any way. You may meet resistance in your request, but do not let it interfere with your ultimate goal of fighting the traffic ticket.

CHAPTER 9

Preparing for the Trial
Step One: Gathering and
Analyzing Evidence

Gathering and analyzing evidence sounds extremely technical and overwhelming, but truly it is not. This is when your folder with all your notes will be important. In some traffic cases, you will have multiple pieces of discovery, evidence, and photographs to keep track of; in others, you will only have a few.

Start by determining how you will stay organized. Use a notebook or legal pad to track all your notes regarding phone calls, requests, and documents you have received. Then, you will start by gathering and analyzing evidence.

Start by requesting discovery — this will show how the officer gathered information in order to issue you a ticket, such as measuring your speed. This chapter will use the specific example of fighting a speeding ticket. You will understand how to interview your witnesses, make the most of your previously taken notes, and learn what the proper use of photos and diagrams are in the courtroom. *The different ways that speed is measured, and each method's margin of error, was previously discussed in Chapter 5.*

Requesting Discovery

This should be your next step immediately after asking for a continuance of your court date. You may submit a request for discovery, which is an official claim asking the court to let you observe the prosecution's evidence against you that will be introduced during the trial. Criminal hearings require both parties to share any information they plan to use as evidence. This allows each side to prepare adequate defenses and acquire proof of any inadmissible details. If your request for discovery is dismissed, the court may believe the prosecution is hiding something from you, so regardless of approval it is a good idea to submit a request for discovery if it applies to your case.

Check with your local court clerk's office to be sure that you have a right to this information. If you do, you must make a specific written request for the disclosure of all notes, documents, and manuals that are relevant to your case. You should send your request to both the police department and prosecutor's office. The discovery will show what the officer will testify to in court.

Discovery gives you a clear idea of what the officer will include in his or her testimony, including the details of how your speed was clocked. Submit your discovery request five days after you receive your ticket so it will already be in the system. The court system is a notoriously slow-moving vehicle, so it might take even longer. However, do not wait too long to submit your request or the judge may deny you based on your procrastination. If your request for discovery comes two weeks or less before your scheduled hearing date, the prosecutor's office may say they do not have the time to put together what you are looking for. Your request should be sent via certified mail so you have documentation proving it was received.

The following is a sample request for discovery. These can get more detailed and complex; however, for a traffic court ticket that you plan to fight yourself, this is a good sample:

Cumberland County District Attorney's Office
City of Portland
123 Main Street
Anytown, ME 01010

January 5, 2008

I, Sam Speeder (your real name goes here), do hereby request the following information in regards to Maine Uniform Summons and Complaint No. 1111-11 issued on December 15, 2007 by Officer John Doe.

1. All notes, records, and log files made by Officer John Doe in regards to the issuance of Maine Uniform Summons and Complaint No. 1111-11.

2. Calibration records for any speed detection equipment used by Officer John Doe in regards to the issuance of Maine Uniform Summons and Complaint 1111-11.

3. All engineering studies regarding the need for a traffic control signal located the intersection of Elm and Oak, the location of which I, Sam Speeder, was ticketed.

4. The Operator's Manuals for any speed detection equipment used by Officer John Doe, in regards to the issuance of Maine Uniform Summons and Complaint 1111-11.

5. The Portland City Police Department regulations and guidelines regarding the use, operation, and policies for the use of speed detection equipment.

> 6. A listing of traffic tickets issued by Officer John Doe for the month of December 2007, to include: date and time issued, alleged violation, and disposition (if determined).
>
> 7. A total tally of all traffic tickets issued by the Portland City Police Department for the month of December 2007, to include: date issued, alleged violation, the badge number of the issuing officer, and disposition, (if determined).
>
> Please mail the requested documents to the address listed above. If there is further need for contact in which written correspondence is insufficient, please call (XXX) XXX – XXXX.
>
> Thank you in advance for your courtesy. Very truly yours,
>
> Sam Speeder

Ensure you list all possible ways you may be contacted so the prosecutor's office can reach you should they have any questions.

Discovery requests are borne by the party producing the documents. Therefore, the driver will not have to pay for these documents. However, if the court says you are responsible for any costs, insist on an itemized bill so you can see the details of what you are paying for. Many state laws provide exceedingly specific limits for costs of copying and for work performed in gathering such information.

Discovery is usually granted within five working days of delivery of the request, but it is not automatically given. So, what if you follow all the steps and your request for discovery is blatantly ignored? Well, for one, you cannot be sure they are actually ignoring you on purpose. Things get hectic at both police departments and prosecutors' offices, and it is possible your request is at the bottom of a pile of files on someone's desk.

If your request is being ignored, be persistent and ask for it again. If the prosecutor will not respond to your requests, the next step is to file a motion to compel discovery. This motion asks the court to issue an order directing the prosecutor to produce the documents requested. Please note, however, that a motion, by its nature, is a contested matter. This means you have to serve a copy of the motion to the prosecutor and give them an opportunity to respond, usually ten to 20 days, in opposition to your motion.

The Basic Goals of Discovery

Discovery is an important part of the traffic court process. It allows each side to obtain information, documents, and other materials to help them determine their strategy. Some of the basic goals of this process are:

- Identify the opposition's testimony

- Find out what documents or other tangible evidence the opposition will use

- Familiarize yourself with your opponent's style, techniques, and character

- Attempt to weaken the officer's testimony using your notes, pictures, and diagrams

- Understand the factual and legal basis of the charge for which you have been cited

What to Do with the Officer's Notes

When you receive the officer's notes, carefully study them. There is a reason officers tend to have perfect memories when they are up on the witness stand — they jot meticulous notes after the incident. That way, he can glance at the notes during the trial and immediately remember what happened at the time.

When you receive the officer's notes, you may re-evaluate your defense strategy or decide the ticket is not worth fighting after all. If you do decide to proceed, you will know what the officer is going to say at the trial. Look for the details in the notes. If an officer has detailed notes, he stands a better chance of proving you were in the wrong. If the notes are not detailed, there is a good chance you can challenge the officer's memory during the trial. The notes should state which lane you were driving in, how the officer recorded your speed, the road and weather conditions, and the traffic patterns. It is also crucial you make note of where the officer was when he observed the traffic violation you were cited for. Did the officer diagram the intersection where you got your traffic ticket? This is common in cases where you are cited for running a red light or making an illegal turn.

Police notes can take a little deciphering. There are times when you jot yourself little notes that make sense to only you. Below are some of the most common notes police officers make on traffic tickets and what these notes mean:

- "S/V" means "subject vehicle," which is your vehicle.

- "D" or "Δ" indicates the defendant, in which case this is you.

- "Est." is an indicator that the police officer visually estimated the speed you were traveling.

- "R" or "r" is a signal your speed was clocked by radar; with any luck, you will find a radar unit serial number noted next to it.

- VASCAR is measured in tenths of a mile, so if you notice a 0.5, it means a half-mile.

- "BUMP" means that the officer bumper paced you. This is an inaccurate method of measuring speed.

- If you see a "Lane 1" or "L1," it is an abbreviation for the lane number; lanes are counted from the center of the road, with lane No. 1 being the first lane and the lane to its immediate right being lane two.

How Your Was Speed Measured

After you see the officer's notes, you should know how your speed was measured. As previously mentioned, there are multiple ways in which to measure a driver's speed. These include:

- Visual estimates — these are usually very inaccurate

- Pacing — the officer maintains a consistent distance between your car and his or her bumper over a specific length of travel

- VASCAR — officer must push two buttons and measure speed from one point to the next

- Radar — the officer may accidentally pick up another car's speed

- Laser — all three beams must be held exactly together to get an accurate reading

- Air patrol — your speed needs to be verified by a ground control officer

- Photo radar — this may be easy to fight, especially if the license plate or the driver of the car is not visible or is blurred

Gathering Your Notes and Research

Start your trial preparation by going back to the notes you took right after the traffic stop. These notes should be extremely detailed because the incident had just happened. If you have not yet taken photographs of the area where the traffic stop happened, now is the time to go back and do so.

Photos

These will prove to be very helpful during the discovery and evidence process and even more so during the actual trial. When you go back to the location where you were ticketed, be on the lookout for obscured traffic signals and signs and actual road obstructions that would reduce visibility. Take the photos at the same time of day you were initially pulled over.

Diagrams

Diagram the road or intersection where you were pulled over. Diagrams are often useful when it comes to making a judge understand what happened, which is one of the reasons so many officers use diagrams in their notes. Your diagram should be detailed but not cluttered.

- Be sure to capture any specifics like direction of traffic, positions of both your car and the officer's car, and any one-way roads or traffic signals.

- Were there any obstructions in the way of the speed limit signs?

- Include the location of stop signs or signals, dividers or traffic islands, crosswalks, limit lines, and the locations of parked vehicles.

- Do your best to accurately capture the approximate widths of the streets and traffic lanes.

- In situations where your speed was measured by bumper pacing, diagram any turns, hills, valleys, curves, and any obvious landmarks in the road.

- You must also note where you first saw the officer and where the officer actually pulled you over. In cases of bumper pacing, the longer the time that your speed was monitored, the more accurate the reading will be.

Do not use ink pens on your diagram. Invest in several colored markers for the task and then choose one dark color — preferably blue or black — to mark all of the roadways and intersections. You can then use the other colors to indicate vehicles and traffic signals that were within the vicinity of the traffic stop.

When you are presenting either a diagram or photograph to the court, you must first ask the judge for permission to do so. Photographs often must be cataloged into evidence. This is also the time when your legal research will be useful. It is extremely important to compare the facts of what happened at your traffic stop to the actual elements of the law that you are charged with.

When you are comparing the elements to whether you violated them, look at it with a discerning eye. As a pro se defendant, it is your job alone to convince the judge that the prosecution has failed to prove you committed one or more of the necessary elements.

Witnesses

Finding potential witnesses can be a tricky process. If you were caught by photo radar, you may be able to see another car's license plate in the picture. If a red light camera caught you, the same may be true. Yet, outside of those two things, it can prove to be exceedingly difficult to find witnesses in a traffic case if you did not have someone with you in the car at the time of the traffic stop.

If you did have someone riding with you in the car when you were stopped, ask that person if he or she will be willing to testify on your behalf in traffic court. Ask to write down their recollection of the incidents the day of the stop. Most people will not have a problem serving as a witness in court, especially if they too believe you were wrongly ticketed.

Interviewing potential witnesses

When you are interviewing your witness or witnesses, be sure to ask for specific recollections of the day. Ask them what lane you were driving in, what the traffic conditions were the day of the ticket, the road conditions, what the officer said when he stopped you, and anything else you think may be relevant the day of the trial. While these questions may seem overly detailed, these will set the stage to question the officer's memory of the day.

CHAPTER 10

Preparing for the Trial Step Two: Organizing Your Case

Start organizing your case. You need to prepare your testimony, witnesses, and questions for both the witnesses and the officer. It will also be helpful to practice talking to the officer. It is important that you address him or her with respect when in the courtroom. You also need to work on preparing for the inevitable cross-examination that will come from the prosecution.

In the United States, you are innocent until proven guilty. While the burden of proof is significantly lower for the prosecution in a traffic case than it would be in a criminal trial, the state must still prove that the offense cited was committed, you are indeed the guilty party, and the time, date, and place of the offense are accurate.

During the trial, the prosecution will present evidence to try and prove these points. Your job is to present testimony and evidence that refutes what the prosecution demonstrates. Remember that traffic court matters are often short and cursory. You may actually have to be quite firm and assertive to convince the court they need to allow you to present your full defense. If you insist on it, you may find yourself faced with a judge who is being impatient with you; do not let yourself be bullied by the judge. It is your right to respectfully question witnesses and the officer who ticketed you.

When your actual trial date arrives, do not let the judge intimidate you. You need to be prepared to explain to the court the significance of the evidence you are seeking to introduce, or what you know you will learn from a particular line of questioning. If the court simply will not allow you to pursue a line of questioning that you believe is essential to proving your case, you must state it for the record that you are trying to establish a specific defense — and name what that defense is. Proceed to explain, for the record, how you will be prevented from establishing that specific line of defense, since the court is not allowing you to do so. You may be permitted to continue, and you are on the record in the event you need to appeal.

Preparing Your Testimony

This part is essential. Defendants who know what to say and when to say it are far more likely to win than those defendants who stand up and hope to come up with a convincing story. Judges are not fond of defendants who walk into a courtroom and declare the officer is lying, it is all a terrible injustice, and the case should be thrown out of court. While drama in the courtroom looks great on television, there is no place for it in real life.

One of the best ways to prepare your testimony for your trial is to practice it. Find friends or family members who will be tough on you and ask them to play the part of the judge. As you present your case, ask them to poke holes in your case by interrupting you with questions as you present your side. It may feel strange to ask a friend to practice with you, but you would be surprised how many people actually enjoy doing this.

Do this until you are fully comfortable answering questions about your version of what happened and the evidence that you will present to back it up. If you feel that the first mock judge is being too easy on you, then ask someone else. You need to be sure you are getting the hardest questions when you are practicing and that you are able to overcome any objection or line of questioning. You have a good chance of winning your case if your mock judge finds you not guilty. If your friend convicts you at the end of your practice session, the judge most likely will too.

A good approach to take when you are preparing your case is to outline your key points on index cards long before your court date. You can do this when you start mock trials with your friend or family members because their line of questioning will often reveal angles you had not thought of. Do these in pencil and leave some space between the lines so you can make more notes as you go along. You will also need the space when it comes to the trial.

Use your notes as you practice making your presentation to your "mock judge." In the courtroom, it is all right to glance down at your notes on occasion, but you should not be reading from your cards or note pad. Additionally, when you are in court, you can use your note cards after you cross-examine the officer who ticketed you. As she divulges her version of the incident, you can jot quick notes on index cards in the blank spaces you left when you originally wrote them. By the time it is your turn to testify, you should be ready to present a smooth and fluid argument that lays out your version of events and refutes the officer's side of the story.

Again, this is why it is a good idea to drop by the courthouse and watch a few traffic court proceedings in action. While it may take a few hours out of your day, it is well worth it. What you learn could be invaluable when it comes to your own trial date. You will get a feel for the proceedings, how the officials act in court, and, if you plan it right, you may even get to see the judge who will hear your case. This is most beneficial because you can get a feel for his or her demeanor well before your trial date. Some judges are pleasant with defendants during proceedings, and others will not even crack a smile, no matter what.

Broad Strategies

You can attempt to demonstrate issues, such as a missing or hidden sign as the cause of your indiscretion and not a willful wrongdoing. Most areas have strict rules about sign placement and road design, so a mistake like this lends to a defense regarding your violation.

This is just one of the several angles you want to consider when defending any position. Before discussing descriptions on possible testimony for each of the potential traffic citations you could receive, you should understand broader defenses that can apply to any of the traffic citations.

In the article, "Five Strategies for Fighting a Traffic Ticket," published by FindLaw, some broad strategies are available to the public. Visit the Web site at **www.findlaw.com** — you will find legal information, lawyer profiles, and different tips to help make the best legal decisions. FindLaw is specifically for the layperson.

Challenge the officer's subjective conclusion

There are many instances when an officer must make a subjective conclusion as to what happened. If you can prove through photographs and diagrams that the officer who ticketed you was not in the best position to accurately see what happened, it is easy to question her subjective opinion in court.

In roughly 20 states across the country, deciding whether it is safe to exceed the posted speed limit is subjective. That is because these states have a presumed speed limit, which means the speed limit posted on the signs are simply a legal presumption as to what is safe for that particular roadway. However, because it is a presumption, the burden rests on you to show that your speed was safe given the conditions that day.

Challenge the officer's observations

Directly challenging what an officer observed is difficult at best when it comes to a traffic trial. In instances where the state's requirement is that the officer actually observed the behavior before giving you a ticket, you need to have an exceptional defense to make a dent in his word. Below are some examples that will help with this feat:

- Witness statements from people who were either with you or observed the incident and can verify your version of events.

- Diagrams that show the court the exact location of your vehicle, the officer's vehicle, and any other important landmarks such as traffic signals or signs.

- Photos of the scene, which may be able to showcase obscured traffic signs.

Prove your conduct was "legally justified"

Suggest that your conduct was legally justified and testify to the fact, that had you not done what you did, more serious damage could have occurred.

Prove that your conduct was necessary to avoid harm

This defense covers unavoidable emergencies that are out of your control. This is effective in instances where you must swerve or speed up to avoid an out-of-control vehicle.

Decide whether any of these possible defenses apply to you:

- "Your Honor, I stopped before the limit line to be sure that I gave the pedestrians plenty of room to cross. Since I had already stopped once, and knew there were no other cars coming, I complied with the law by actually stopping prior to entering the intersection."

- "From where the officer was sitting, there was a large hedge obstructing his view." A photograph taken from where the officer had his car parked will help. The photograph, in conjunction with your diagram, shows that the officer would have been physically unable to see you stop at the stop sign.

- When you entered the intersection, the traffic light was still yellow. When you went back several days later to watch the intersection, the light going northbound turned green before the light headed eastbound turned red. The officer cited you for running a red light because from his vantage point, his light was green. It would help to obtain sworn statements from other drivers traveling through the intersection the day you went back to observe.

- Review the photographs from the red light camera. If you cannot see the driver's face, you have a solid argument it was not you. "I was not in town that day and all members of my family drive this car. While I am the registrar of this vehicle, I was not the driver."

Illegal turns

Some defenses of these may include:

- Review the state's definition of what constitutes a "business district." Was it in fact one of these when you made the U-turn? If not, your case may be dismissed.

- Although in a residential district, there was no oncoming traffic, therefore, the U-turn could not be considered unsafe.

- If the sign that prohibited a U-turn on the highway was obstructed, the case may be dismissed. Go back to the location and take a picture of the exact location of the U-turn.

Unsafe lane changes

Some defenses of these may include:

- You did make a left-hand turn with oncoming traffic, but based on the distance between your car and the closest oncoming car, there was plenty of time to safely make this turn. The car in the oncoming lane did not have to swerve or apply his brakes. The officer who ticketed you was behind, not in the oncoming lane. Due to this fact, your vehicle obstructed his view of the events. Therefore, he was not fully able to judge the distance between your car and the oncoming car.

- You were backing down the road because a car was driving uncontrollably toward you in the same lane — there was nowhere to go but backward.

Right-of-way violations

This is when you fail to give another motorist or pedestrian the right of way. If the officer shows up to court for this hearing, you need to have the best possible testimony prepared. These are the types of incidents officers diagram and take meticulous notes about. As a result, the officer will likely remember the incident in exceptional detail.

- Although the other driver was to your right, he waved you through the intersection and you then proceeded with caution and reasonable safety. From where the officer was parked, he would not have been able to see the other motorist waving you through the intersection.

- Upon approaching the four way stop, you entered the intersection first, therefore, you departed from the stop first. From the angle at which the officer was parked, it would have been impossible for him to fully distinguish which driver entered the intersection first. Photographs from the spot the officer was parked in would help — ask permission to submit these for evidence.

Exceeding "absolute" speed limits

In states with an "absolute" speed limit, you should focus your trial and testimony preparation on arguing that you were not speeding at all. Remember, "absolute" speed limits mean there is no room to negotiate or launch a defense that you were acting "reasonably safe."

- If the officer used radar to clock your speed, you may be able to use this defense: If there was other traffic traveling in the lanes next to you, at the distance from which the officer clocked your speed, his radar beam would have been about three lanes of traffic wide. The officer's beam could have picked up the speed of the vehicle on either side of your car.

- "I was on an extremely curvy road, Your Honor." If the road was not straight and the officer paced your car, the officer could not have accurately paced you because the peaks and valleys would not allow him to keep a consistent distance between his bumper and yours.

- "Your honor, while I admit that I was speeding, my conduct was legally justified. Had I not exceeded the speed limit to pass the truck in front of me, my car would have been hit by large pieces of construction debris flying out of the back of the truck. This was hazardous and could have caused a serious accident."

Exceeding the "presumed" speed limits

This is the speed limit you would much rather be arguing about. Since you only need to prove that you were operating your vehicle with reasonable safety, you should focus your testimony and trial preparation on arguing that you were not speeding, but even if you were, you were only going a few miles an hour over the speed limit, and the speed you were going was safe given the conditions.

- "The time at which I was ticketed was at 6 a.m. on a Saturday." If possible, argue that the time you were driving was early in the morning on a weekend. If the road was straight and there was no other traffic on the highway, you could have operated your vehicle with reasonable safety although you were traveling above the speed limit.

- "Even if I did exceed the speed limit, I did not exceed it by more than five miles per hour." If you did not exceed the speed limit by more than five miles per hour, it is usually a good defense — this is usually not seen as unsafe speeding.

General speeding defense

Another option is to attempt to fight your speeding ticket with math.

On December 10, 2007, The National Motorists Association (NMA) published an article titled "Fight Your Speeding Ticket with Simple Math." The article was in response to the large number of motorists who were ticketed as a result of "being clocked with devices that measure how fast a vehicle covers a known distance." The NMA breaks down how to beat your speeding ticket with simple math in a few easy steps. Before you know the math, review the few basic facts. These break down how much distance a car traveling 60 miles per hour will travel in 1 hour, 1 minute, and 1 second.

We know that 1 mile equals 5,280 feet, therefore:

- A vehicle traveling 1 mile per hour will take one hour to cover 5,280 feet, or 1 mile

- There are 60 minutes in one hour, so a vehicle traveling 1 mile per hour will travel 1/60 of the 5,280 feet per minute. This is equal to 88 feet per minute.

A car traveling at 1 mile per hour will travel 1/60 of the 88 feet that it covered in one minute. This is equal to 1.47 feet per second.

These numbers are important to know because you will reference these when you do the math.

- Based on the above facts, a vehicle moving 1 mile per hour will cover 1.47 feet in one second. To figure out how far a vehicle will travel at a specific speed, multiply that speed by 1.47.

  A car driving 60 miles per hour will cover 88 feet in one second (60 x 1.47 = 88). This number is slightly rounded from 88.2.

- Now you can determine how many seconds it would take a vehicle to cover a set distance at a certain speed. Divide the set distance by the speed and then divide that answer by 1.47.

- A car that travels a distance of 500 feet at 70 miles per hour: Divide 500 by 70, which equals 7.14. Now divide

7.14 by 1.47. You now know that this car will cover 500 feet in 4.9 seconds.

At this point, you are wondering how these math equations may help you during trial. When you are cited for speeding and you were clocked with VASCAR, you should get a description of the distance over which you were clocked, how long it took your vehicle to cover that distance, and the speed you have been charged with traveling.

Based on this information, you can either prove or disprove the accuracy of the VASCAR citation. If the citation claims you covered 300 feet in 4.2 seconds and you are being charged with speeding at 60 miles per hour in a 50 mile per hour zone, you can quickly prove the citation is unwarranted. Here is how:

- At 60 miles per hour, you would have traveled about 370 feet (88 feet per second x 4.2 seconds)

- At 50 miles per hour, you would have traveled about 309 feet (73.5 feet per second x 4.2 seconds)

Based on this knowledge, you can argue in court that you were indeed traveling within the posted speed limit of 50 miles per hour. You should then ask that your case be dismissed, as this evidence is clearly not accurate.

Preparing your testimony for trial is not difficult. Take the time to look at exactly what you have been charged with. Take out your notes that have the elements laid out, piece by piece, and focus on any element of the law you answered "no" to. If there are elements to the law that are marginal and you feel like you have not totally violated them, you can also focus on those.

The more you practice and prepare your testimony, the more confident you will appear in the courtroom. This is to your benefit.

Preparing Your Witnesses

Getting your witnesses ready for trial can be an easy task. You will want to review the events of the day and be sure that you agree on what happened on the day you received the ticket. You will need to prepare your witness to be cross-examined by the prosecution. This should not be extremely difficult, considering the more relaxed atmosphere of traffic court.

It is in everyone's best interest if your witnesses are at your mock trial with the mock judge. Have another friend play the prosecutor and have them question your witness. Be sure to go through it until your witness is comfortable with the questions.

If you can get them to agree to it, have them go to the courthouse and watch a trial in progress with you, just so they can observe how the proceedings work. You can assure them that, in the grand scheme of things, being a witness in a traffic case is far easier than being one in any other type of trial.

Also, it is important to note you need to prepare your witness to be subpoenaed. A subpoena is a document that orders a person to appear for a trial. These documents must be personally delivered, in hand, to the witness, and also the appropriate witness fees. A witness fee is a statutory requirement in some states to compensate a subpoenaed witness for her time and travel. For example, California requires a party subpoenaing a witness to pay that witness $35 per day and $0.20 per mile traveled. It is important to note, though, these fees only apply to subpoenaed witnesses. If you can convince the witness to appear voluntarily, then no fees apply.

Subpoenas must be issued within two weeks or more before the trial.

Preparing your questions for the witnesses

What are you trying to accomplish at your trial? It will help to answer this by thinking about what you received a ticket for. Tailor your questions for your witnesses around that. Using the example of exceeding the presumed speed limit, here are some of the questions you can ask your witnesses:

- "Can you please tell the court what the traffic conditions were on the day that this traffic ticket was issued?"

- "Can you please tell the court if there were any other vehicles on the road at the time of the traffic stop?"

- "Can you please tell the court what time of day the traffic stop occurred?"

- "Was the road on which you were traveling straight?"

- "Did you personally feel as though the speed of the car was unsafe or unreasonable given the current conditions that you have just described?"

Given the road conditions, time of day, and actual structure of the road, you were traveling at a safe and reasonable speed. Prepare your witness for the court date by letting him or her in on your defense strategy. Then, just as you have already done, you need to elicit the help of stern friends. Ask them to be the judge and practice your defense with your witness. Go through all your questions. If the prosecution asks your witnesses if they have discussed the testimony with you, they can answer honestly and say yes. They just need to make it clear it was only because they were nervous about the events of the day. The only potential issue may be discussing testimony you have already given with another witness who has yet to take the stand.

Organizing witness testimony

If you have more than one witness, write down all of their names, what their respective roles in the case will be, and what each will say and how their testimonies will help your case. You need to decide in what order they will testify to help present the most logical series of events. Be cautious, though. Sometimes, a friendly witness will offer to bend the truth for you. Be aware that perjury, or lying under oath, can put that witness in jail. In Oklahoma, for example, perjury is a felony punishable by up to five years in prison. Moreover, an adept prosecutor can tell when a witness is lying. This can destroy the plausibility of everything the witness has said, even if the bulk of it is true.

Prepared and organized witnesses are far more persuasive that those who are not. Begin by familiarizing your witnesses with the various legal facets of the case and the strategy of your defense. His or her testimony should bolster one or more key points. Just like you did with your own testimony, practice before a friend who acts as a judge, and have your witnesses rehearse.

Subpoenaing witnesses

A "subpoena" is a document that requires a witness to be present at the time and place of your trial. If the witness does not appear, he or she can be arrested, fined, or put in jail for contempt of court. The court clerk must issue a subpoena in a traffic case if you request it. Rules and procedures regarding how to go about this vary from court to court. Be sure to ask the court clerk how a subpoena is to be prepared and served.

If the witness was a friend or family member, he or she will most likely agree to appear in court without a subpoena. In the case the witness is a pedestrian or another driver, you will want to serve him with a subpoena informing him to come to your trial. Please note, however, that you cannot serve the subpoena yourself. Although rules differ from state to state, parties to an action are not permitted to serve subpoenas. Rather, you must enlist another person to serve for your subpoena. Generally, anyone over the age of 18 will do. Also, many states, like New Mexico for example, will have the sheriff serve for you. Ask the clerk of your court for the rules for your jurisdiction. The following are three situations where a subpoena is essential in prompting a witness to appear in court:

- A student who will serve as a witness needs to be excused from school

- A witness does not want to appear, but you feel if she is subpoenaed, she will testify on your behalf

- A witness has offered to testify but is unreliable, and you think he or she may forget to appear if not subpoenaed

Remember, it is not a good idea to subpoena a hostile witness. Someone who is opposed to appearing in court will most likely not make a good witness. He or she may even damage your case. The exception to this rule is when you think you cannot win without this person's testimony. If you think he or she will tell the truth under oath, subpoena him or her.

Preparing for the Prosecution's Cross-Examination

A prosecutor's job is to cross-examine you and anyone else who testifies on your behalf. If a prosecutor is not available, the judge will ask the officer if he wants to cross-examine. Most officers will decline this offer. In this event, the judge may ask questions.

The aim of cross-examination is to find holes in your story and the testimony of your witnesses. Remember the following when you or your witnesses are cross-examined:

- Stay polite and professional. Do not answer in an evasive, hostile, or argumentative manner.

- Keep your answers succinct, so they answer the questions posed to you instead of volunteering information that may hurt your case.

- Do not be deterred from elaborating on yes or no questions. For example, if the prosecutor asks you how fast you were going and you reply 60 miles per hour in a 55 miles per hour zone, you might add there were no cars so you felt it safe to do so. If the prosecutor tries to cut off your explanation, you should reply, "I believe a have a right to explain as part of my answer. May I continue?"

- Tell the truth. This might sound obvious, but many people try to stretch the truth. Prosecutors are skilled at exposing lies, especially if they sense you are not giving the whole truth.

If you do not know, say so. Many people fear appearing ignorant and harm their testimonies. For example, if your witness was busy and did not notice whether two cars turned ahead of you on a yellow light, but can testify you crossed the limit line when it was still yellow, make sure he or she knows it is acceptable to respond "I don't know" when he or she does not.

Occasionally, a friendly witness will volunteer to stretch the truth a little bit, just to help you — this is never a good idea. As previously states, lying while under oath is a felony charge called perjury and your witness could go to jail over it.

CHAPTER 11

Preparing for the Trial Step Three: The Officer's Testimony and Cross-Examination

Now that we have discussed how to organize your case and subpoena witnesses, we will discuss the next important facet in organizing your case — the officer's testimony.

Normally, the prosecution's case consists only of the testimony of the police officer who wrote you the ticket. The testimony will often sound like this: "I was in my parked patrol car when I saw the defendant drive through the intersection at Main and High streets, heading south on High Street after the light turned red. The traffic was heavy and many cars had to brake to avoid an accident. The road was also wet due to a rainstorm."

Listen carefully to the officer's testimony and concentrate on ways to challenge his testimony. Depending on what he says, it may be possible to legally object to the officer's testimony so it can be removed from your trial or cross-examine the officer to poke holes through his testimony to bring doubt to its truth and accuracy.

Objecting to Testimony

Objecting to testimony is a practical decision. Ask yourself, "What are my chances of success?" Also, consider how harmful the testimony is to your case. For example, if the officer is providing information about the weather and it is irrelevant to your offense, you will achieve little by objecting to that information even if it is correct.

On the other hand, objecting to a police officer's testimony can throw him off balance and disconcert him. The effect would be to weaken his testimony and weaken the case.

The officer's notes

After writing your ticket, most police officers will take notes of what happened on the back of the ticket. They do this in case there is a trial. These notes are not admissible in court in most states. It is technically improper in most states for the officer to read them unless he follows essential procedural steps, which lawyers call "laying a proper foundation." The officer must testify that he:

- Cannot remember all the details of the violation

- Wrote them down shortly after writing the ticket

- Needs them to refresh his memory

Because most recipients of tickets never object to reading these notes, most officers do not know how to adhere to these procedural steps, known as laying the proper evidentiary foundation. This affords you the opportunity to object to the officer reading the notes. Ask the judge to consider informing the officer to follow the proper procedure.

If the officer is able to lay the foundation for reading the notes, then the judge should direct the officer to allow you to see his or her notes. If the judge does not, ask the judge to direct the officer to allow you to see his notes. After you receive his notes, carefully review them, but do not hand them back to the officer if the officer has not created the proper legal foundations for utilizing them. When the judge asks you to return them, renew your "hearsay" objection and request that the officer testify based on his or her "independent recollection" — without reading the notes. You are victorious on two fronts even if the judge allows the officer to utilize his or her notes:

- You have read the officer's notes if you had previously been denied.

- You can declare in your closing argument that the officer has a bad recollection for events and cannot contradict any evidence you set forth, which should raise doubt concerning your guilt.

You should also raise an objection if the judge "coaches" the officer. Sometimes a judge comes to the aid of a confused officer who is trying to lay a proper foundation for getting around the hearsay rule and using his or her notes. If the judge does this, you may wish to raise your objection politely again by saying, "Objection, Your Honor. With all due respect, it seems that the court is aiding the officer in testifying by leading him on with questions. I again request the court to merely instruct the witness to testify by memory or lay a proper foundation for the inclusion of this written documentation." At that point, the judge could permit your objection. The judge will demand the officer to lay a proper foundation or overrule it. In either case, you have succeeded in making your point and can move on.

When facts are assumed as evidence

Another improper tactic that officers sometimes utilize when testifying is to say they saw your vehicle (the "defendant's" vehicle) go through a stop sign or other such infraction. In this case, the officer is connecting you to what she observed by looking at a vehicle, which may not have been yours — essentially assuming facts as evidence. This type of objection would be vital if your defense rested on the officer identifying the incorrect car.

The correct way for the officer to testify is to say she observed "a vehicle" rather than "a defendant's vehicle" commit an infraction, and she pulled over the vehicle and identified you as the driver by requesting a driver's license. When you permit the officer to identify the vehicle as the "defendant's" vehicle, you have permitted her to improperly establish the vehicle she saw as actually being the one you were driving.

You should object to the officer's "assuming facts not in evidence" or "lack of personal knowledge" by stating, "Objection, Your Honor. This testimony assumes facts the officer has not testified to. No evidence exists before this court as to who owned or drove the vehicle the officer declares to have observed. The officer could not possibly possess personal knowledge of the identity of the owner of the car she merely sees driving on the street. I move that her testimony not be admissible."

The judge can sustain, or grant, your objection and then "strike," or disregard, the officer's testimony. The judge can also request the officer to "rephrase" her testimony, sometimes coaching the officer to say that she initially saw the vehicle and then identified you.

Hearsay evidence

In most states, hearsay evidence refers to when an officer or any witness testifies to something she did not personally observe. Reading notes from when the officer issued the citation is one type of hearsay. Hearsay is an out-of-court statement offered for the truth of the matter. Although at first glance an officer's notes might not appear as hearsay, in fact they are. The notes are statements of the officer made out of court (here, in the form of a writing) seeking to establish that you committed a traffic violation. Such testimony is normally not allowed, and you are permitted to make an objection. If the officer wants to establish that you committed a traffic violation, she must testify to it in court. She cannot rely on her notes to establish it. If a prosecutor's question calls for hearsay, you should immediately say, "Objection, Your Honor. The question calls for hearsay."

Note that there are several exceptions to the hearsay rule, which permit specific types of hearsay to be considered by a judge or jury. The most common one permits an officer to testify to any statements you made that would tend to prove your guilt. For example, the officer asks you, "Do you know why I stopped you?" and you answered, "Because I was speeding."

Although an examination of the admissibility of evidence goes beyond the scope of this book, it is wise to be prepared to object to two of the most common situations, in which hearsay occurs:

- When an accident happens. In this case, you should object if the officer, who probably was not a witness to the accident, tries to testify to what another individual involved in the accident or an eyewitness told her. Again, according to the hearsay rule, an officer can only testify to what she observed, not to what was told to her by other people.

- For speeding violations involving air patrol measurements. Object if the officer in the patrol car tries to testify what an officer in an aircraft said your speed was. The officer must testify according to what he observed and not what the aircraft's officer observed. Both the aircraft officer and the ground officer must testify at your hearing.

As an example, say your car hits another at an intersection guarded by four stop signs at each entrance. You tell the officer you entered the intersection first, and the other driver ignored the stop sign. Based on the declarations of the other driver and pedestrian, the officer concludes you were at fault for neglecting to yield to the car to your right. You contest the ticket and go to trial. In court, the officer is there but neither the other driver nor witness appears. When the officer testifies what the driver and witness said about the accident, you should promptly state, "Objection, Your Honor. That's hearsay. It should not be admissible." The judge should agree by saying, "sustained," which strikes the statement from the record. The prosecutor can subpoena a witness to testify directly, but prosecutors do not usually do this in traffic court.

Cross-Examining the Officer

As we have previously discussed with cross-examining witnesses, preparation is vital to successfully questioning or cross-examining the officer. You must keep in mind you are trying to raise a reasonable doubt as to your guilt. You may ask almost anything as long as the answer you desire is pertinent to your attempt to prove you did not commit a specific element of the violation. Structure your cross-examination step by step, starting with the least vital background questions, and finishing with the ones that go to the crux of your defense.

Be careful. If you do not have a particular reason to ask a specific question, do not ask it. Unfocused questions do not usually result in answers that will aid you with your case, and they usually give the officer an opportunity to repeat damaging facts. In addition, do not include an admission of guilt in your questions, such as, "Where were you when I ran the stop sign?" Be non-committal, and change the construction of your question to "Where were you when you claimed I ran a stop sign?"

Again, be prepared with your cross-examination, but be flexible enough to alter your questions in response to the answers that the officer will provide. Jot down a double-spaced list of questions, and take it with you to court. Edit these questions, adding and deleting as the trial progresses. Keep in mind that you want to tailor your questions to the officer's response. Pay close attention to what the officer says. For example, if the officer's answer is evasive, ask more specific questions until you get the answer you want.

Ask specific questions. Avoid questions such as "What happened next?" or "Why did you stop me?" The officer then has the opportunity to harm your defense by answering, "You broke the law." Include in your question a form of self-defense, such as "Is it not true that there was a hedge of bushes between where you were parked and my car?" or "Is it true you stopped me because of a radio report from an aircraft clocking my speed, and you did not observe my speed yourself?"

Your goal is to demonstrate to the judge and jury the following:

- The officer's powers of observation were flawed

- One or more legal elements of the specific offense are lacking

- That a defense exists

- The officer was preoccupied and doing several things at once

- The officer might have lost sight of your car between the time she saw the infraction and the time she pulled you over

Obviously, you may hear a surprising answer. When you do, you must depend on your broad understanding of the facts to determine if you wish to ask more specific questions or quickly alter your line of questioning.

Keep in mind that you should never argue with the officer. Do not adopt an antagonistic attitude toward the officer. It simply is not advisable to argue with her. Even in the case when the officer fabricates a lie or gives an absurd answer, you should rationally and politely ask more questions and do not reply, "That is just not true."

Let us look at some examples that differentiate between arguing and making a valid point:

Your question: Officer, how close to my car were you when you first took your radar reading?

Officer: 500 feet

Argument response you should avoid: "You know very well that the radar beam width at that distance cannot tell the difference between cars in different lanes. Your testimony is a falsehood."

Valid response: "Officer, you previously testified that your radar unit has a beam width of 6 degrees. Is it accurate to say that at 500 feet from your radar gun, this means the beam will be more than 100 feet across?"

In your second response, you are less emotional than in your first response. You are also using the legal vernacular of the court. You may want to follow up with a statement such as, "On the road where I was ticketed, aren't the individual lanes much narrower than 50 feet?" Here you are supporting your case with facts, while not personally attacking the officer.

An officer's non-responsive answer

When you are successful at asking the officer a succinct question whose truthful response might be damaging to the prosecution and bolster your case, the officer might try to avoid the question by changing the subject or being evasive. If this is the case, request the judge to order the officer to provide an answer to your question.

Cross-examination differs from court to court. If there is a lectern, you might cross-examine from there. On the other hand, you may be requested to pose your questions from the table where you are sitting. Just be sure to stand up when you cross-examine, as this will keep you focused. Never walk up to the officer unless you want to bring up something in his diagram, chart, or notes. In this case, you will be expected to ask, "Your Honor, may I approach the witness?"

For example, a motorcycle officer pulls you over for a speeding infraction. If he was not wearing eye protection, you want to prove that he could not accurately see your vehicle because the wind or debris was blowing into his eyes. After this initial argument, you will close by saying he may have lost sight of the vehicle committing the infraction, thereby pulling you over instead of a similar-looking car.

Your cross examination: Is it true, Officer, that you were not using any eye protection while you were riding your motorcycle on the day you issued me the ticket?

Officer's non-responsive answer: Well, I could see, and the windshield on my bike...

Your response to his non-responsive answer: Your Honor, I object. The officer's answer does not respond to my question. I ask that the witness be asked to answer my question.

Besides non-responsive answers, officers may go on tangents about how bad your driving was. Obviously, this can be damaging to your case. When this happens, simply say, "Your Honor, I ask the court to tell the witness to confine his answers to my questions." There is a fine line between going on a tangent and explaining your side. If the witness is talking about something totally unrelated to your question, then it is appropriate for the judge to ask the witness to confine his answer to the subject of the question. However, if the witness is still on topic, just because he is adding more that you want, does not mean you get to stop him.

The officer's power of observation

The officer's perception is the foundation for nearly every traffic prosecution. If you can prove that the officer cannot see beyond 100 feet, and your infraction occurred at 200 feet, you should win your case. Yet, it is not only the officer's hearing or sight that is in question. Trials usually occur one or two months after the fact, and the officer has handed out several tickets since then, therefore, his memory of the event is often a big issue at the trial. The better job you do at establishing that he or she does not recall the where, why, and how the incident occurred, the more doubts you can raise as to the truth of his testimony.

Sample Questions

Some sample questions are included below that test the officer's knowledge of the location and conditions where he or she observed you. Remember to keep it lively.

Your initial questions should be constructed to get the officer to admit he was performing many tasks at the same time besides observing you. These could include starting the car, driving, speaking on the radio, and so on. The more activities the officer was doing, the less likely he was able to observe how you were driving.

- Where were you when you spotted my vehicle?

- Where did you initially see my car?

- Was your patrol car or bike moving or stationary at the time?

- Was your engine idling or was it off?

- What did you do to start the vehicle?

- Were your lights on?

- Was your two-way radio in use?

- Did you start your car just before you say you saw the infraction or while it was happening? (If just before, you can argue that he made up his mind to stop you before the fact. If during, he might have been too pre-occupied starting the car to see you well).

- In which lane were you driving?

- In which direction were you driving?

- What was your speed? (If you were stopped for speeding, leave this out. You do not want the officer to say he drove 80 miles per hour to catch you.)

- Was your view of the road clear when you say you saw the infraction?

- Besides my car and yours, were there any other cars on the road? If there were, the less he remembers about the other cars, the more your argument is bolstered by his lack of memory. On the other hand, if he remembers the other cars vividly, you may be able to assert that he was busy observing every car and he would never be able to observe yours accurately at the same time.

- Describe the vehicles in front of your vehicle.

- Describe the vehicles on either side of you.

- How fast was the traffic flow?

- Did you see my vehicle passing any others?

Utilize the officer's answers to frame further questions. For example, if he says you passed other vehicles, ask for details such as type of car, color, and make. He probably will not be able to remember. If he says other cars were slower than yours, but also says you were not passing other cars, he is committing a contradiction that you can include in your closing argument.

Ask questions about road conditions:

- Officer, is it true two lanes existed in either direction?

- Is it also true there are islands to divide opposite traffic directions? Is it also true traffic islands prevent collisions with traffic from the other direction?

- Is it true there were no sharp curves where you say you observed my speed?

- Is it true there were no gullies or hills in the area?

- Were there railroad crossings or not?

- Were there road repairs or not?

- Were there any obstructions or not?

- Were there any soft shoulders or not?

- Were there any spilled liquids or not?

- Were there pedestrians, bicycles, or animals?

In questioning the officer, your strategy is trying to prove the officer's memory is poor — this means the court may doubt the accuracy of his testimony. In this respect, it is wise to ask questions you know the police officer will not be able to answer. The best way to do this is to look at his notes beforehand, which is known as "discovery." *This was discussed earlier in Chapter 10.*

"Discovery" is a process of gathering evidence. The legal system is compelled to provide information about your dispute, to respond to questions, and to produce documents before your case goes to trial. Handled in the proper manner, discovery can be vital and essential in preparing a successful case.

Normally, the objectives of formal discovery are:

- To disclose evidence that is favorable to your story

- To disclose the evidence that your adversary, in this case the officer, is likely to offer against you if the case goes to trial

- To lock the officer into a story before trial, so that you can question the plausibility of witnesses who testify at trial to different stories or facts

- To familiarize yourself with the officer's style, techniques, and character

- To get relevant, admissible evidence such as documents, admissions, testimony, and physical evidence

- To identify the officer's lay and expert witnesses and to establish what his testimony will be

- To comprehend the factual and legal basis of the officer's citation

Four elements of discovery are open to you as a defendant in most jurisdictions:

- Request for admissions

- Interrogatories

- Depositions

- Notice to produce

You may serve the request for admissions. It is a written request for the admission of truth. It is basically a set of questions that can be answered by true or false. It must be filed on time.

Interrogatories are simply questions from one party to the action to another party. For example, an interrogatory question in a speeding case might be along the lines of, "describe the weather at the time the officer issued you a ticket." If you receive an interrogatory, it is your duty to answer the questions truthfully, accurately, completely, and precisely. The same goes for any party to whom you issue interrogatories.

A notice to produce is utilized to obtain documents or items a party believes is relevant to the lawsuit and will be helpful during discovery. This is the most relevant element of discovery for your case. This might occur at a mutually designated place where you can read the evidence and take notes or copy it. The documents can then be used in court to bolster your case or help you prepare your cross-examination.

A deposition is an oral examination of any party or person before a court reporter. The cost and time required for a deposition usually precludes it from use in a traffic infraction trial. Interrogatories are a more convenient version of this, but have the drawback of not allowing you to follow up on an incomplete or evasive answer with another question.

There are alternatives to fighting your traffic ticket in court — it is known as "trial by declaration" and is basically a mail-in trial. The defendant writes out an argument and mails it to the judge.

You can ask for this option from the clerk or at the arraignment (the hearing where you enter a formal plea — guilty, not guilty, or no contest). However, this is not a recommended way to go because there is a good chance the officer may not appear in court and you miss the opportunity to cross-examine him if he does.

CHAPTER 12

Preparing for the Trial
Step Four: Going to Court
for the First Time

In 26 states, you do not have the right to ask for a trial by jury for a traffic violation — this means a judge decides your verdict. The other 24 states allow you to ask for a jury trial for a traffic violation. However, if you exercise this option, you will probably encounter a group of very irritated people who had to take time off from their busy schedule to sit in on a traffic violation. They might be wary of your motives in requesting a jury trial and hold it against you. Moreover, in a jury trial, a prosecutor is assigned who may make your experience more difficult than going up against an officer in traffic court who does not have as much courtroom experience as a prosecutor. If you decide on a jury trial for your traffic violation, then hire a lawyer. Non-jury trials are fairly informal. This chapter discusses what is likely to occur with and without a prosecutor.

The Courtroom

Traffic court trials take place in courtrooms. A judge, a clerk, and a bailiff will normally be at the trial. The clerk is seated at a table immediately in front of the judge's seat, the bench, or to the side. Her job is to supply the judge with essential files and documents and to ensure the proceedings go smoothly. There will be either a court reporter present who records a word-by-word account of the case or the hearing will be electronically recorded.

Arrive early to the courtroom for your trial. Once you enter the courtroom, inform the clerk or bailiff you are there, and take a seat in the spectator section. Courtrooms are separated about two-thirds of the way to the front by a wooden divider known as the "bar." The judge, court personnel, lawyers and you (when your case is announced) utilize the area in front of the bar. Others who are waiting for their case to be called, or the general public, are seated behind the bar. When your case is announced, leave the spectator section behind the bar and enter the area where the judge and court personnel sit. You will be seated at one of two counsel tables placed directly in front of the bar, in front of the judge.

In informal courtrooms, witnesses follow you to the counsel table. At more formal trials, they remain behind the bar along with the police officer. They advance to the witness stand once their names are announced. If you visited the courtroom as recommended in the previous chapter, you will be acquainted with this procedure. You and your witnesses will be sworn in either before the judge arrives or just before testifying.

Be courteous and respectful to all court personnel, especially the judge. This might be difficult if you have a problem with the legal system and feel you have been wrongfully cited with the traffic ticket. However, if you are angry or hostile toward the judge, he or she will likely hold it against you. It is vital to the judge for you to separate your emotions from the facts of the case. Address the judge as "Your Honor."

Trials without a prosecutor

Many states conduct traffic court trials without an assistant district attorney or prosecutor — attorneys for the state. When the clerk announces the case, the police officer presents his testimony asserting your guilt. Afterward, you have the opportunity to cross-examine him or her.

When there is no prosecutor, the judge will permit the officer to relay his story in narrative form, maybe interjecting to pose questions. You then, with your notes and mental preparation, have the chance to cross-examine him or her with your own questions.

Sometimes, a judge could offer you to waive your right to cross-examine the officer. The judge might not offer you the opportunity or will advise you to skip this step. Insist on your right to cross-examine the police officer. This is your chance to test him on his recollection of the facts of the case, which might cast doubt as to your guilt.

After cross-examining the officer, you have the opportunity to present your side of the case and bring in the testimony of your witnesses. The judge may ask questions at any time during the cross-examination or presentation of your or your witnesses' testimony. Then, the judge declares his or her verdict — guilty or not guilty — and announces the appropriate fine.

Some judges may speed you through the process or question you directly along with the officer. Be prepared for this behavior. You can do this by visiting the courtroom to observe how the judge conducts his or her courtroom. You can then develop a list of the important points of your defense that must be included at the trial. If the judge interrupts, you can look at your list and say, "Your Honor, I have prepared a few concise points that are critical to my case, and would like to be permitted to present them to you." Most judges will yield to this polite request.

Trials with a prosecutor

In some courts, a prosecutor will undertake the state's case. If so, the proceeding will have a more formal tone. Each side will present its respective testimony with an opportunity for cross-examination and the trial will have an opening and closing statement. Theoretically, you have the privilege of presenting an opening statement before the officer testifies and a closing statement after all evidence is made. If there is no jury, the judge may advise you to waive these procedures. If you wish to see if a prosecutor is handling the case, visit the courtroom or call the clerk's office beforehand.

Requesting a continuance

Before the trial begins, you also have the opportunity to request a continuance. *This was previously discussed in Chapter 9.*

The following are some reasons to delay the court date:

- You require more time to get organized.

- You or a witness will be out of town.

- You need to delay the time of your possible guilty conviction to keep from acquiring too many "points" on your license over a particular time frame.

To postpone your trial, prepare your written request for continuance at least one week or more in advance of the date of the trial. Send the document to the police officer and any prosecuting attorney. You can find the officer's name on your ticket. The clerk of the court will have the contact information for the prosecutor. If you make a continuance on the day of the trial, it will most likely be denied. However, if you make it several weeks in advance, it will most likely be granted, as one delay per trial is usually granted.

If you do not obtain an answer before the trial date, call or visit the clerk. If the continuance has not been granted, it is advisable to appear in court on the scheduled date to determine whether the continuance has been granted. Be prepared to go to trial on that day despite the fact you plan on requesting a continuance. If you present proof you attempted to contact the officer and the prosecuting attorney, your request will probably be granted. If you are going out of town and cannot appear in person, contact the judge directly either by fax or priority mail. Reference your earlier written request together with supporting documents, and ask for an urgent postponement.

Arraignment

All is well and good when you have decided to fight the ticket, and prepared your case. But when you receive a traffic ticket, you have several options.

Arraignments are utilized by the court to state what you are charged with, as well as list your basic legal rights: the right to an attorney, to cross-examine the officer, to call witnesses to testify for you, and in some states, to request a jury trial. The bottom of your ticket includes the location of the municipal or justice court and a date. You must appear at the court on or before that date and plead either guilty or not guilty. If you plead not guilty, go straight to the clerk, plead not guilty in writing, and request a trial. The other option is to attend an arraignment.

Some of your basic rights include the right to:

- A trial at which the state has the burden of proving you are guilty beyond doubt.

- Hear, see, and cross-examine the officer's witnesses.

- Call or subpoena witnesses who testify to your innocence.

- A court-appointed lawyer if your offense, such as drunken or reckless driving, is punishable by jail time. In some states, you will actually not go to traffic court — you will have to be tried at a higher court.

- A jury trial if the state permits it.

Here, many things can occur. You will enter a plea — "guilty," "no contest," or "not guilty." If you plead guilty, the judge will calculate a fine and you will remit it. The DMV will list this as a conviction and your insurance rates may rise according to your provider. If you plead no contest, the same procedure occurs. Use this plea when your ticket was written as a result of your participation in an accident. A "no contest" plea will stop whoever you were in an accident with from utilizing your plea as evidence in a civil suit against you. With this plea, you are not admitting guilt.

Pleading 'not guilty' will allow you a trial and you will pay bail. The bail amount is usually the amount you would owe on the ticket and is the court's way to ensure that you show up for trial. If you end up winning your case, though, the court refunds the bail money. If you lose the trial, you lose it.

You can then decide if you want a formal or informal trial. Whichever you choose, ask for a trial where the officer acts as the prosecutor. This is your legal right. After all, it is your objective to have the officer not show up so the case gets dismissed. Again, like in the case of a regular trial, observe an arraignment before you actually are arraigned so you can follow and be familiar with the proceedings and the judge.

Many courts have completely eliminated the arraignment process by which you enter your plea before a judge, but in other courts, you have the privilege to insist on entering your plea in court — just ask for it. The following are reasons why you would want to enter a plea in court:

- At an arraignment, you can inquire about your right to "discovery" or obtaining the evidence the officer will use against you at the trial.

- You can ask for a jury trial, if your state permits it.

- This is where you can plead 'no contest' to a violation resulting from an accident. Remember, the only time this really makes sense is if the ticket stems from a traffic accident. If you plead guilty, then this counts as an admission that is admissible in a civil trial. For speeding or other offenses, it does not make too much sense.

To facilitate court time, a judge may recommend that you choose a court trial. A court trial or a bench trial simply signifies a trial before a judge, instead of a jury. If you reside in a state that permits jury trials, reply by saying, "No, Your Honor, I want a jury trial."

Do not be talked out of your right to a jury trial. If you do your homework for the more complicated jury trial, you have a better chance of winning in traffic court in front of a jury than before a judge. Jurors often feel they have been treated unfairly in traffic court and will be more sympathetic to you. Also, a prosecutor might dismiss the case if you opt for a jury trial, especially if the case is weak. Moreover, the prosecutor may allow you to attend traffic school and answer to a reduced plea.

Speedy trial rules

Under the Sixth Amendment of the United States Constitution, you are guaranteed "a speedy and public trial" in all criminal cases, but the amendment neglects to say exactly what "speedy" signifies. Many states have laws defining that term. For example, California necessitates that a case be thrown out if not brought to trial within 45 days of entering before a judge a "not guilty" plea.

Where your state's speedy trial period is short, a judge may ask you to waive your right to a speedy trial. This is oftentimes done at an arraignment when you request a motion for discovery. He or she will ask, "Do you waive time for trial?" If you enter a not guilty plea with a clerk's office in California, for example, the judge will ask you to sign a form sacrificing your right to a speedy trial in exchange for skipping the arraignment process. In other states, you may have the option of waiving time. If you are asked to "waive time," ask the clerk if you have the option of refusing without having to go to the arraignment. If so, you should say, "No" because in busy courthouses, your trial will be set toward the end of the time permitted by law. This means if the officer does not show up for the court date and the judge does not dismiss the ticket, she will have to reschedule your trial with the officer present before the "speedy trial" deadline. This may be impossible — in which case you win.

Settling Your Case

Jury trials can be drawn-out for you, judges, prosecutors, and the police. This motivates all concerned to settle your case before going to trial. The situation dictates what type of deal can be made. For example, if you were ticketed for speeding and running a stop sign, the prosecutor might offer that she would drop one charge if you plead guilty to another. If you are attempting to lower the points on your license (or one violation permits you to go to traffic school and another does not), this could be a major compromise you would go for. In yet another case, the judge may permit you to go to traffic school to maintain a clean record.

Negotiating

Nothing stops you from going up to the prosecutor to determine if she wants to make a deal to avoid a jury trial. Negotiations in jury-trial cases can occur in many different locations, at a formal "pre-trial" or "settlement" conference in the judge's chambers, on an informal phone call, or before trial in a hallway outside the courtroom. The location of the negotiation matters less than the outcome — a better deal than if you went to trial and received a guilty verdict. Be aware, it is unrealistic to expect to get your case dismissed. Available options include:

- Permitting you to enter a guilty plea for a less-serious offense than you were charged with. For example, you could accept a guilty plea for "simple" speeding as opposed to driving 30 miles over the speed limit.

- Dropping one violation for a guilty plea to the other charge. For example, dropping the charge that you changed a lane unsafely and did not stop at a signal in exchange for admitting guilt to a speeding charge.

- Negotiate a deal where your conviction will not involve a high fine or suspended license. For example, in a circumstance where you ran a red light and would be fined $400 with a suspended license, you can negotiate for a $100 fine with no suspended license.

- Sending you to traffic school so the offense will not appear on your record.

Remember the following points when negotiating:

1. Be cautious regarding consenting to plead guilty to several offenses in exchange for the promise of a lesser fine. A jury trial lined up may give you more bargaining power. When the prosecutor will not drop at least one charge in exchange for pleading guilty, you should go to trial.

2. Do not be intimidated by a difficult prosecutor who presents you with a "take-it-or-leave it" offer. A gentle "no" on the first round will usually result in a better offer later.

3. Do not expose your strategy to the prosecutor. When negotiations do not succeed, you will leave yourself vulnerable in the courtroom. Just say you believe you can present a very strong case for your innocence. If the prosecutor knows his case is weak, he will be willing to negotiate.

4. Never admit guilt to a prosecutor or police officer before you make a deal. Be aware of informal gatherings in the

hallway or before the trial where a prosecutor or officer may ask you, "Just between us, you were going 80 miles per hour, right?" If you admit your guilt, the statement can be used against you in court.

5. Never make a deal on trial day until you determine whether the officer will be present. When the officer is not there, the judge will probably drop the case. The prosecutor, knowing the officer will not be there, may offer a generous settlement. You should then ask him if the officer will be there or stall for a few minutes to see if the officer shows up. If he still does not show up, decline the offer.

Making the deal

If the prosecutor and you arrive at an oral agreement, you must then appear before the judge. The prosecutor will then inform the judge that, for example, you have agreed to plead guilty to a lesser charge in exchange for the dropping of a more serious charge. Sometimes, the prosecutor will recommend a sentence.

Despite the fact that the judge does not have to agree to your agreement, he or she usually approves it. If the judge does not approve the agreement, you should withdraw your plea and go to trial.

CHAPTER 13

Preparing for the Trial
Step Five: The Trial Date

Preparing for trial often means preparing or building evidence for your case. There are many methods you can use to establish your position. Clear pictures and diagrams can be helpful so long as they prove your innocence. Do not assume the judge or jury understands them. Be prepared to explain everything. *Methods to establish your position were discussed in Chapter 9.*

Build evidence for your case as early as possible. If you have been in a car accident, immediately document with notes what just occurred. Follow these steps:

- Take notes.

- Take pictures if you have a camera. Use them to locate trees, street signs, light poles, bushes, curbing, other vehicles, and so on.

- Interview witnesses and get names, phone numbers, and addresses.

- Examine the attitudes of witnesses to determine whether they are sympathetic to your side.

- Get insurance information and driver's license numbers.

- File the information, and obtain a police report when available.

- Get appraisals if there is damage, such as street crossing guards, paramedics and so on.

As a general rule, the sooner you collect evidence before the trial date, the better off you will be in terms of having a strong case. Three categories of evidence are allowed in the courtroom:

- Oral testimony: This is the most common form of evidence. It can be your testimony or a police officer's or a witness's.

- Documentary evidence: This category includes written forms of documents, printed materials, photocopies, photographs, and recordings.

- Real evidence: This category includes tangible items that are relevant to the case.

Your Testimony

If you have not made an opening statement at the beginning of the trial, be certain to make it before your testimony. Then, your testimony in a jury trial should proceed like in a bench trial. Look at the jurors and make eye contact. You want them to see you as an honest, law-abiding citizen who has been wrongly accused.

- While the judge usually remains stoic during trials, jurors do not. Observe jurors for non-verbal signs and reactions during your testimony to determine if you are getting your point across or just confusing them.

- When your testimony is finished, and after the prosecutor has cross-examined you, present your witnesses.

- Your witnesses can testify in a narrative fashion or in response to guiding questions from you. If the judge suggests you question the witnesses, you may say you are unfamiliar with the manner in which such questions should be asked, and would like your witness to proceed in a narrative fashion. If the judge declines your request, be prepared to ask your witness questions.

Cross-Examining for Particular Infractions

Cross-examining the officer is one of the most important facets of the trial. Cross-examining the officer should be aimed at weakening his testimony on the specific facets of the offense you are charged with. Therefore, the questions you ask should be geared toward the violation for which you got the ticket. For example, in a speeding citation where the officer measures your speed with a radar gun, you might want to question the officer's ability to use his radar gun. Leading is all right on cross-examination of the other side. You cannot ask leading questions of your witness, just the other side's witnesses — here, the officer.

The following are cross-examination questions that are used for specific violations.

Visual speed estimation

When an officer judged your speed merely through visual observation and not with pacing, radar, laser, or VASCAR, you should question him as follows:

1. "What length of distance did you observe my car?" If it was a short distance that you can substantiate with the location of a tree or traffic light, you can argue he could not be accurate to observe your speed over such a short distance.

2. "Did my speed vary after you observed me?" If he says you slowed down after seeing the officer's car, you can argue that the original high estimate was accurate only over a miniscule distance, and consequently, it is an unreliable observation. If the officer says your speed suddenly increased or decreased, ask where. He probably will not be able to remember, which may cast doubt on his testimony.

3. "Was my car moving toward you, from you, or across your line of vision?" You should include presented evidence on this point. You can then say in your closing argument that it is more difficult for the officer to gauge the speed of a car moving in a direct line toward or away from him than when the car travels across his direct line of vision.

4. "Have you ever been involved in controlled examinations where you were asked to gauge vehicle speeds?" Most officers will respond negatively to this question — a point you can deliver in your closing argument. When the officer responds yes, you can ask whether he always guesses the right speed. If he responds yes, it may be a lie and if he responds no, you can point out how hard it is to accurately gauge speed.

Speed gauged by pacing your car

Pacing, you may recall, occurs when an officer estimates your speed by looking at her speedometer while following or "pacing" your car. Ask the following questions if this situation is the case:

- "For what distance did you follow my car?" If the distance is short, you have a good case that the reading was inaccurate.

- "Did you maintain a steady distance between my car and your car?" If she answers yes, she may be mistaken because she had to close in on you to pull you over.

What she wants to say to prove her case is the distance was identical over the entire time you were paced, at which point she sped up to stop you. If she denies that she sped up to stop you, ask:

- "Did you observe your speedometer while you were pacing me?"

- "How often did you observe it?" If she responds that she was constantly watching it, ask, "When pacing at a set speed, is it important that you watch the alleged vehicle continuously?" If she says no, then ask:

- "If you do not watch a vehicle continuously during pacing, can you lose track of the car you are pacing and focus on another vehicle instead?" If she denies the necessity of watching a vehicle continuously, question her methods of pacing in your closing argument.

- "Was there other traffic?" Ask this only if you know for a fact there was.

- "Where were the other cars?"

- "Describe the other cars."

- "Were you focused on the other traffic to drive safely?"

- "How often did you observe my vehicle?" When she replies that she was observing her speedometer carefully and is able to testify as to the other traffic on the road, ask these follow-up questions:

- "So you were observing other vehicles and mine at the same time as your speedometer?" If she replies no, she was mostly observing your vehicle. Ask again, "And you were watching other traffic too, correct?" Then, you can make the point in your closing argument that she was too busy observing other traffic and your car to look at her speedometer.

- "How close to my vehicle were you when you were pacing me?" If she was pacing more than a few hundred feet, ask:

- "Do you agree that the capability to pace is contingent upon good depth perception, so that you are able to follow at a constant distance?"

- "Do you also agree that the farther away an object is, the harder it is to pace it?" If she replies no, ask her what method is more accurate, a 100-foot pace or a mile behind?

- "Have you recently taken a controlled test where you paced a vehicle at a known speed from [whatever distance she claimed she paced you from]?" The response will usually be no.

If the incident in question took place at night ask the following:

- "Officer, did you pace my vehicle at night or dusk?"

- "Would you say that it is more difficult to maintain a constant distance to execute an accurate pace at night than during the day?" She will probably agree. Otherwise, ask the following:

- "Is it not more difficult to truthfully pace at night when you can only see two taillights as opposed to during the day when the entire car is in view?"

In order to question the accuracy of her speedometer, you should ask:

- "Before you cited me with a violation, how long had passed since your speedometer was last calibrated?" If the officer replies that it was accurate, she may be avoiding the question and you should ask again. If a speedometer has not been calibrated recently (say, within the past year), you can use this fact in your closing argument.

- "Do you have a record of the most recent speedometer calibration with you today?"

- "Did you know that speedometer accuracy is affected by tire circumference?"

- "Did you also know that tire circumference is affected by tire pressure and wear?"

- "Then, is it now fair to say that speedometer accuracy is affected by tire pressure and wear." She will probably agree. If he does not, ask:

- "When you have worn-down or low-pressure tires, the odometer would read high, agree?"

- "Were your tires examined when your speedometer was calibrated?"

- "Were they examined when you cited me for the violation?"

- "Did you know that a tire's air pressure is related to its temperature?"

- "Have you rotated the tires on your patrol car or have they been changed since the date of the last calibration?"

These questions are all designed to question the accuracy of the officer who observed you speeding. They should be used during cross-examination to bolster your final argument. They also question her ability and methods of findings. Do not be intimidated, but always be polite.

Speed gauged by aircraft

There are two methods for an officer to estimate your speed from an aircraft:

1. By timing the transit of the vehicle between two points on a roadway.

2. By using ground markers and a stopwatch to discover how fast the aircraft is moving and then using the aircraft to pace the vehicle below.

Contingent on which method is utilized, your cross-examination should normally try to cast doubt on:

- The validity of the timing method the aircraft officer utilized to time the movement of your car — or the aircraft — across highway markings.

- The ground officer's awareness of the distance between highway markings. Keep in mind that if this knowledge is based on what she was informed by the airplane officer, it is "hearsay" evidence and you can object.

- The precise identification of your vehicle by the aircraft officer.

- The ground officer's correct identification of your car from the aircraft officer's description.

- The precision of the timing of the movement of either the vehicle or the aircraft across the two highway markings.

The following questions should be asked of the aircraft officer regardless of the method utilized to measure your speed:

- "Officer, you used a stopwatch or other timing tool to measure the movement of the aircraft or vehicle between the two highway markings, right?"

- "Did you time the movement of the aircraft/vehicle [depending on which method used] over a fixed distance?" The answer will usually be yes.

- "Did you actually measure the distance between the highway markings on the ground?" If the answer is no, request the judge to "strike" the officer's previous statement. Say, "Your Honor, I move to strike the officer's testimony, since it was based on a distance divided by time that was not known by the officer." If the judge upholds the strike, you have won your case because there is no other evidence to justify your speeding. But, if the judge refuses, you must continue.

- "Did you observe my car continuously without looking away?" If she responds yes, ask:

- "Did you use a log and stopwatch to record my speed?" If she responds yes, ask:

- "Did you not look down at them and enter records in your log?" The point you wish to deliver is if she was doing more than one thing at a time, she can easily lose sight of a specific car. Therefore, if she responds yes, ask:

- "Did you report other speeding vehicles at the same time?"

- "How many vehicles were you observing?"

- "Over what distance did you monitor my car?" If she watched your car over a short length, for example one-tenth or one-fifth of a mile, ask:

- "Could you declare once more the time it took my car to travel between the two points?" Then ask:

- "If because of normal reaction time, you did not start the stopwatch until my vehicle passed over the first mark (0.5 seconds), the true time my car traveled between the two markings would have been 6.5 seconds. And at one-eighth of a mile or 660 feet and 6.5 seconds, the true speed would be 69 mph" (660 feet/6.5 seconds = 102 feet per second or 69 mph). Use this formula only if the officer established the aircraft speed by using the markings and "paced" your car from the air in the airplane.

- "Is it not true you established your aircraft's speed in this manner before you finally established my car's speed?"

- "How much time elapsed between the time you calibrated the speed of the aircraft and when you paced my car?"

- "If a headwind hampered your aircraft when you timed its passage between the markings, would you not have to fly again between the markets to establish your slower speed in relation to the ground?"

- "Did this happen?"

- "Are you sure the wind speed did not affect your aircraft?"

- "What point on the aircraft did you utilize to determine the aircraft speed?"

- "How far from you was that point?"

- "If your head moved forward or backward while watching the reference point pass between the first and second markers, the elapsed time on your stopwatch would be inaccurate, correct?"

- "When you identified my car, you did not identify it by reading my license plate, is that true?" (From 500 feet in the air, this would be nearly impossible.)

- "You did not call down the make or model of the car did you?" Ask this only if it is not mentioned in the officer's log. It usually is not because an officer cannot get this information from 500 feet in the air.

- "Was there other traffic in the form of other cars?" If yes, ask:

- "Could you describe the make and models of the other cars?" This usually is beyond the memory scope of the officer, which you can use in your final argument to cast doubt as to the memory of the officer and her testimony to your guilt.

- "Did you report other vehicles besides mine?" If she says yes, you can argue her attention was divided among many cars and she could have possibly mixed up the speed of your car with that of others.

- "Is it not true you were first alerted to my car only because of the radio report from the aircraft?" Ask this question and the following question if the officer in the air radioed to the officer on the ground. If she says yes:

- "Then your knowledge of the speed was determined specifically on the radio report." If she says yes, this is hearsay evidence and you should ask the judge to strike the testimony. Even if the judge denies it, you should argue in your closing statement that the ticketing officer gave you a ticket based on secondhand information, which is often inaccurate.

VASCAR

Below are specific questions to cross-examine the officer who ticketed you using VASCAR. *VASCAR was previously discussed in detail in Chapter 5.*

When the officer utilized VASCAR to establish your speed, your goals during cross-examination are the following:

- Her reaction time might have been slow, thus clocking too short a time and too high a speed.

- She may have had trouble viewing the stop or start point, therefore mistiming your speed.

- While moving, the officer might have operated the unit wrong when having to press the buttons four different times during traffic.

The following questions should be asked to cast doubt regarding whether the officer pushed the buttons at the right times:

- "How distant were the two points that my vehicle passed through?"

- "How many seconds did you measure my car passing between the two points?" If the two points were less than 500 feet apart, the time should be five to ten seconds. If the officer's response falls within five to ten seconds, ask the next eight questions marked by bullet

points, in this section Otherwise, skip to the ninth bullet
point, and continue questioning from there.

- "Could the time that elapsed when you pressed the time
  or distance switches have been a factor in monitoring
  my speed?" The officer will probably say no, explaining
  that she did not when the car passed the points, but
  when she anticipated the car passing the points.
  If so, ask:

- "But, if when I went past the first marker, you had not
  guessed accurately, and instead reacted after my car
  went past the point, then the time measured would
  actually be a little short, correct?" The answer should be
  yes. If she says no, ask:

- "Assume that if, when I drove past the first point, you
  reacted and pressed the time switch 0.5 seconds later.
  Would my time be low?" If she says yes to this
  argument, ask:

- "And given the above circumstances, would my speed be
  wrongly miscalculated?"

- "Let us assume you had reacted instead of anticipated.
  Your reaction time when I drove past the first point
  took 0.5 seconds. Now you testified that you calculated
  my time between the two points as, for example, three
  seconds. So, is it not accurate to say that the true time
  passage is 3.5 seconds?"

- "At, for example, 200 feet and, for example, 3.5 seconds, that is an average speed of 57.1 feet per second, correct?" Offer the officer to utilize a calculator.

- "And to determine miles per hour, you divide feet per second by 1.47, correct?"

- "And 57.1 feet per second divided by 1.47 comes to 38.8 mph, correct?" Obviously, these figures are just examples. Next, your primary objective is to question the officer's capability to precisely observe when your car passed the second point.

- "How far from the two markings were you located?" She will most likely answer that she was closer to one than the other.

- "Therefore, is it not true that it was easier for you to hit the time button when my car passed over the nearer point?" If she hesitates at this question, continue with:

- "Is it simpler for you to press the hit button at the proper second when a car is 50 feet away than when it is half a mile away?"

- "Have you recently undergone a controlled test of your ability to judge when a car has passed over a half-mile away?" The answer is probably no.

- "Is it not also true that if you misjudged when my car passed the distant point, that your reading would be inaccurate?"

- "And consequently, that would prove that your VASCAR reading of my speed was inaccurate?" If the officer concedes these points, it is wise to quit while you are ahead. You can utilize these admissions as part of your final argument casting doubt on your guilt. If you continue with more questions, the officer may withdraw or qualify your admission by saying you were going so fast that the speed would more than compensate for the margin of error of a VASCAR reading. Next, we will concentrate on the fact that an officer must execute four time-and-distance switches in a very short time, which is something that is very difficult.

- "To use VASCAR correctly, you must press the time switch twice and the distance switch twice while moving, correct?" The answer will be yes.

- "And that adds up to four operations, right?"

- "And it would be inaccurate if you wrongly pressed the distance button at precisely the point where your car passed the beginning and end points, right?"

- "And the same holds true in relation to calculating my vehicle passing the two points when you had to push the time button, right?"

- "And if you performed these four operations in the incorrect order, an erroneous reading would occur, right?"

- "And you had to do all four operations accurately over what time period?"

Radar

When the officer used radar to calculate your speed, you can ask the following questions. Your objective is:

- To prove she does not understand how radar works.

- To prove she was not prudent about retaining her unit's accuracy.

- To prove the speed she measured may not have been yours.

Ask the following questions, in the case where the officer did not give you the radar readout at the time you were cited:

- "Does your radar contain a control that permits you to lock in the targeted car's speed on a readout?" If she answers yes, then ask:

- "Did you give your unit's speed to me when you stopped me?" If the answer is no, you can assert in your final argument that since she could have shown you your speed, there must be some reason she did not.

- "Could you tell me how speed-determining radar works?" If she is unable to do this, consider this lack of knowledge as part of your closing argument.

- "Isn't it true that sensitive instruments, such as radar, must be calibrated before and after every shift to assure their precision?"

- "Did you calibrate your radar before or after you calculated my speed?" If she answers no, use this assertion in your final argument. If she asserts yes, ask:

- "How did you calibrate the radar exactly?" If she replies she turned on the unit's calibrate switch:

- "You did not use a tuning fork?"

- "The radar unit's manufacturer recommends calibration with a tuning fork, don't they?"

- "Is not utilizing an external tool like a tuning fork certified by a testing laboratory as a better way to test a unit's accuracy than an internal device, such as a switch?" If she replies she used a tuning fork:

- "What was the certified speed for the tuning fork?" If the speed is much different from the speed she clocked you at, ask:

- "Is it not true that calculating radar accuracy with a turning fork at one speed is not a sure thing at a different velocity?"

- "When was the tuning fork last calibrated by a testing laboratory?"

- "Do you have a certificate attesting to this tuning fork's accuracy?" And irrespective of what calibration method was used, ask:

- "Has your radar unit ever broken down in any way?" If no:

- "Then it has never been fixed or taken to the shop to your recollection?" If she says no, ask:

- "You mean not even for a routine check-up, which is every six months?"

- "What's the optimal range of your radar unit?"

- "When you aim your radar at a close object, the antennae will pick up signals reflected from other sources, correct?" If yes, ask:

- "Were you aware that a more distant but larger vehicle may reflect a stronger signal than a smaller nearby car?" And if it was windy the day you were cited, ask the following:

- "Have you ever gotten a false speed reading by incorrectly aiming a radar unit at another car or a tree blown by the wind?"

- "And if those items are in motion, can you obtain a wrong reading?"

- "Can tree limbs or leaves blowing in the wind reflect radar signals that result in false readings?"

- "Can dust or rain generate false readings?"

- "Are you aware of harmonic frequencies?"

- "Did you know harmonic frequencies of nearby citizen band radio sets, for example, can influence radar and cause false readings?"

- "Are you aware that power lines or transformers can influence radar and cause false readings?"

- "When you first calculated my speed, were you observing it with your naked eye or with radar?" If with naked eye, then ask:

- "Consequently, you had already made up your mind that I was exceeding the speed limit before consulting your radar?" If the officer was looking at your car, then ask:

- "So, you had already assumed I was speeding before taking a reading." If the officer was consulting the radar, then ask:

- "So, you had already made up your mind about my speed before looking up at my car."

- "Can an untrained person use radar?" The answer is no.

- "Please describe your radar training."

- "How long ago were you trained?" In New Jersey, for example, officers are required to train every three years.

- "What was the duration of the training?" North Carolina, for example, requires officers to take a 40-hour course.

- "Did a radar salesperson administer this training?"

- "Did you receive on-the-job training in radar?"

- "Have you participated in any tests where you determined a car's speed by radar and then measured it with the actual speed?" This occurs almost never.

Laser

When you cross-examine an officer who used a laser gun, you want to establish the following:

- The officer does not know how to use it.

- The unit might have been incorrectly used.

Questions to establish these inaccuracies include:

- "How does a laser work?"

- "The laser works by measuring distances, right? It uses the speed of light and the time it requires a reflected beam to return between the unit and the vehicle, correct?"

- "How many measurements of distance does it make in a second?"

- "Does the laser unit emit three separate light beams? And each beam hits a different spot on the car?"

- "In addition, when you aim the unit to obtain an accurate reading, you must aim it at the same spot on the vehicle during the entire time?"

- "If, over the measurement period, you initially aim at the passenger area, then move the gun slightly so the beams hit the hood, then at least part of your measurement will take into account the difference between the location of these points?"

- "Have you read the manual for the radar unit and are you acquainted with it?" If yes, ask:

- "Does it mention this type of inaccuracy?"

- "Could it be possible you committed this type of error?"

- "Was there other traffic in my direction?"

- "Is it not also possible for one of the three beams to reflect off a vehicle near mine, going at a different speed, with another beam reflecting off my vehicle, affecting your laser gun with an incorrect result?"

- "Is it also possible for a laser beam to hit off a vehicle that was passing me resulting in one of the three beams hitting my car while the others hit the adjacent car?" If she says that is unlikely, then ask:

- "Isn't this type of error covered in your instruction manual?"

Running a stop sign

This type of case almost always depends on the officer's word against yours. There are two basic defenses geared at raising a reasonable doubt as to your guilt. They are:

1. Whether you arrived at a total stop behind the "limit line" or the imaginary line that would be drawn at the corner.

2. Whether there was a regulation stop sign controlling traffic in the direction you were going.

The questions you ask the officer are contingent on where she watched you. If she testified she was situated on a cross street or on the other side of the intersection, not at the entrance to the intersection, inquire:

- "Were there other vehicles in front of you when you observed my car?"

- "How many vehicles were in front of you when you observed my car?"

- "Describe them." She may not be able to.

- "How far down the street were you?"

Running a stoplight

The defense for this violation is simple. As it is permissible to enter an intersection on a yellow light, your task during cross-examination is to cast doubt on the officer's accurate observation that the light was indeed red when the front end of your car crossed the "limit line" or cross street.

- "Did you observe my car at the time the green light first turned to yellow?" If she says she did not, question her ability to see you run the red light when it is cast because she could not observe that so quickly.

- "For how many seconds does the yellow light stay on?" If she does not know (they are typically between four to six seconds, but you should time the one you were ticketed for running to find out for sure), ask:

- "Can you guess how long the yellow light was lit?" If she still does not answer, you can argue in your final argument that her observation powers are not that good. If you were not speeding, ask the following questions:

- "Was I traveling at or near the speed limit?"

- "What was the speed limit?"

- "How far was I from the intersection when the green light turned yellow?"

- "What is the general stopping distance at that speed limit?" The point of asking these questions is to establish that if you were going the speed limit, the length of time of the yellow light was too short to permit you to come to a definitive stop before the yellow light turned to red. If the officer was perpendicular to you, she probably guessed that when she saw the red light change to green, the yellow light changed to red in your direction. If this is true, ask:

- "Could you observe the color of the light facing me from where you were parked?" Go on, only if she says no.

- "Why do you say I entered the intersection on a red light if you could not observe the red light from where you parked?" She will say her light was green.

- "You assumed my light turned from yellow to red at precisely that time?" She will probably say yes.

- "Did you then examine the signal to establish whether the light in my direction was synchronized so that mine turned red when yours turned green?" Very few officers check the lights for this. You can argue there is no way of really knowing whether the light was red. This argument is bolstered by the fact that since the officer was perpendicular to you, she could not see that well. If the officer was situated at another difficult angle from you, ask:

- "How well could you see the color of the light from where you were parked?"

Illegal turns

This chapter will now discuss defenses for tickets for making unsafe turns. When an officer tickets you for an unsafe turn, it is usually based on a subjective opinion unless there is a sign posted that prohibits the turn. If the turn was at an intersection, ask the following questions:

- "Was the intersection governed by a traffic signal?"

- "Did you observe the signal's color when I entered the intersection?" She could only have seen the signal if she was directly behind you.

- "Did I completely stop in the intersection before making a turn?" Ask only if you did. It proves you were cautious.

- "Was my turn signal flashing?" Ask, only if it was on.

- "For how long?" The standard is 100 feet before you turn.

- "Did any vehicle blow its horn when I turned?" Ask only if they did not.

- "Did the oncoming vehicle slow down because of my turn?" She will probably answer yes.

- "Did that car screech its tires?" Ask only if it did not.

- "Could the vehicle coming from the opposite direction have slowed down because the driver was waving me to turn?"

- "Is it not correct to say that many safe drivers slow down at an intersection out of safety reasons, whether or not someone up ahead is turning?"

When the officer does not show up

One of the foundations of the criminal justice system is that you have a right to confront your accusers and cross-examine them when you are charged with a crime, even a minor offense such as a traffic violation. When the officer does not show up, you should present this point to the judge — that your right has been denied and your case should be dismissed. Lawyers refer to this situation as a "dismissal for lack of prosecution." Make the judge aware of the inconvenience you have suffered as a result of the officer's failure to show up in court.

You can say:

"Your Honor. I move that this case be thrown out. I am prepared to proceed to trial. I have subpoenaed two witnesses, both of whom are in the courtroom. We have each taken a morning off from work at considerable cost to defend this case. I received no notice in advance from anyone that the case would not go forward. Obviously, if I failed to show up and the officer was present, I could not have the right for a last-minute postponement. Therefore, I respectfully request that the court dismiss this case for lack of prosecution and in the interest of justice."

The above request to dismiss is usually granted by the judge. The judge will deny your request only if the officer has communicated a meaningful reason for not showing up and informing you. Excuses such as law enforcement and medical emergencies are reasonable excuses. Unacceptable excuses include vacations, training, or medical leave because these events are known in advance, and you would have been able to be notified.

CHAPTER 14

Bench Trial: What to Expect

There are two types of trials for traffic violations: 1) Jury trials, and 2) Bench trials, or trials presided over by a judge. This chapter examines the bench trials.

The Clerk Calls the Case

Your trial starts with the clerk calling your case, by stating, "State of California" v. "your name." Assuming you and your witnesses have already been sworn in, you should move to the front of the courtroom and sit at one of the two tables facing the judge. Whether you stand or sit when you present your case depends on the design of the courtroom and the judge's preference. Most courtrooms contain a traditional witness box adjacent to the judge's bench where you and any witnesses — including the officer — will testify. Many judges, though, have you and the officer present your cases from the counsel tables. When cross-examining each other, you simply turn to face each other from your respective tables.

The clerk or the judge, once you are all seated, then states the bare facts of the case. She may state: "You are charged with a violation of Chapter 7 Section 22351(a) of the Vehicle and Traffic Law of the State of California, by driving 65 miles per hour in a 40 miles per hour zone on the 150 block of Ventura Boulevard."

Last-Minute Motions

Motions are requests made to the judge before the prosecution makes its case. Depending on the facts of the case, they include:

- Asking for a continuance, if you require more time.

- Asking for a dismissal of the case for prosecution's failure to disclose officer's notes as per your written request.

- Asking the judge to order the prosecution to give you a copy of the officer's notes so you can prepare for the trial.

- Asking for dismissal, if the prosecution has taken too long to bring the case to trial.

To make a motion, simply stand up after the judge stops speaking and declare, "Your Honor, I would like to make the following motion." Afterward, contingent upon the motion, state: "I move to dismiss this case based on the fact that the prosecution has neglected my written request to discover the officer's notes. I have a copy of that request dated January 25, 2008."

You would make a motion to dismiss the case if the officer does not show up. You would also make a motion to exclude multiple witnesses from the courtroom at the same time. For example, sometimes the prosecution has more than one witness. This occurs during aircraft-patrol situations where one officer from the air testifies and one officer from the ground testifies. This can also occur when two officers working in tandem pulled you over and cited you. Moreover, if you were involved in an accident there may be neighboring witnesses who will testify against you.

You do not want to permit two or more prosecution witnesses in the courtroom at the same time testifying against you because they can coordinate their stories against you. If each officer witness testifies outside the presence of the other, you can check for inconsistencies in their stories. To exclude multiple witnesses, simply ask the judge, "Your Honor, I request that multiple witnesses be excluded from the courtroom." The judge will normally grant such requests, and such a motion is not deemed aggressive or hostile.

Requesting a continuance is another type of motion requested by you of the judge. This motion asks for a delay for whatever reason. *This was covered in Chapter 13.*

Opening Statements

Before testimony is given, both the prosecution and the defense have the opportunity to make an opening statement going over the violation and declaring how they intend to prove each facet of the case. Realize that in doing this, you do not have to provide proof at this point. You are merely presenting your case and laying the groundwork later for your potential witnesses and for cross-examination of the officer.

When the police officer shows up and the prosecutor does not, it is even more rare for the prosecution side to deliver an opening statement. This is due to the fact most officers realize their function is to produce evidence, not to act as an advocate for a guilty verdict or suggest to the judge how to interpret the testimony.

A prosecution's opening statement

"Your Honor, the People (or State) will show through the testimony of Officer Jones of the Jonestown Police Department, that the Defendant, [your name], was operating a blue 1995 convertible, where the speed limit signs posted 35 miles per hour. It will also prove that Officer Jones, depending upon his radar speed detection device, established [your name] drove more than 60 mph, and he confirmed for more than half a mile that [your name] was going in and out of traffic."

Your opening statement

You have the legal privilege of presenting an opening statement before the prosecution testimony or to "reserve" the right to make it until just before you start your defense. In many courts, the judge will think you do not want to present an opening statement and will request the prosecutor or police officer to start their testimony. At this point, you should interrupt and state, "Your Honor, I would like to reserve the right to make a very brief opening statement until before I testify."

You may ask, why should you wait to present your opening statement? By waiting, you have the chance to gear your remarks to what you learn in the officer's testimony. Moreover, by not presenting your opening statement at the start, you avoid giving away your strategy in advance. Keep in mind that even when the prosecution does not present an opening statement, you have the right to present yours. You might have to request the opportunity from the judge though. Do so by speaking up politely.

The Prosecution's Testimony

After the opening statements are presented, the officer who gave you the ticket will explain why you are guilty of the violation you were cited for. During most informal traffic trials, the officer will testify by standing behind the counsel table. In more formal trials, he will testify from the witness stand beside the judge.

When no prosecutor is there, the officer will state what happened and why he believes these facts were justified in issuing you a citation. You have the opportunity to interrupt the officer's testimony, but only if you identify a valid legal reason to "object" to a particular aspect of his testimony. You must politely state, "Objection, Your Honor," and then explain the legal foundation for your objection. Never let your emotions get the best of you. Remain calm and rational.

Be advised that you should not object frivolously, especially in a bench trial before a judge. The judge surely is aware of the rules of evidence far better than you are and is likely to disallow any testimony or documents the officer sets forth that are way out of bounds.

The Four Grounds for Objections

The first ground for objection is the witness has not provided enough detail to prove he has personal knowledge of his testimony. This is often referred to as "failing to provide a foundation or legal basis" for the testimony.

For example, when a police officer refers to a diagram, he must first state how he is sure the diagram is a precise representation of the place you were stopped or ticketed. Usually, this is accomplished when the officer testifies that he created the diagram after writing the ticket while still observing the scene of the infraction. If he neglects to say this, you can declare, "Objection, Your Honor. The officer has not provided a proper foundation for utilizing the diagram. He seems to have no memory of the incident and should not be permitted to refresh his memory with the diagram that may not even be of the correct location."

This objection can be helpful if you think the officer really is not prepared to lay the proper foundation, in which case the diagram cannot be used against you. But if you are fairly certain the officer will simply explain facts and persuade the judge his diagram represents precisely the area the ticket was given, it is an error to waste the judge's time with will likely be deemed a trivial objection.

Sometimes, the officer provides evidence at the trial that you never got. In this case, say, "Your Honor, I object. The officer is utilizing his notes, a copy of which I asked for via discovery many weeks ago. I have a copy of my written request that I would like to present to the court now. It was never responded to. I therefore request that this evidence be stricken from the record along with his testimony."

Give a copy of your written request for discovery to the clerk who shows it to the judge. If your objection is upheld, or "sustained" by the judge, ask for a continuance to review the notes. If your continuance is granted, the officer will have to return to court another time, which he may not be able to do. If this happens, the case will be dismissed. In the worst-case scenario, the judge will give you time to look at the notes at that time, which can help you effectively cross-examine the officer. If the notes are sloppy but the officer admits he needs them to refresh his memory, you can claim he cannot remember details that are not included in his notes — details that can exonerate you.

The goal here is to discredit any information the officer does not cull himself, so in your final argument you can cast reasonable doubt as to your guilt. For example, if the officer says another pedestrian after an accident told him you were driving fast, you will want to object. You will say that this "hearsay" evidence does not prove you are guilty of speeding.

If the judge sustains your objection, the officer will have to start all over again and explain exactly how he knew you were the driver of the vehicle. He will have to describe the vehicle, how he pulled it over, and how he checked your identification to determine it was you. He may have trouble doing this if your car escaped his sight briefly or else he may be thrown off by your objection. If the judge overrules your objection, allow the officer to testify again.

Your Cross-Examination

- Be polite and do not argue.

- Ask simple questions that require short and direct answers.

- If his answer surprises you, do not argue.

- Do not ask open-ended questions that give the officer an opportunity to tell a long story.

- If he does that anyway, interrupt by saying, "Thank you, you've already answered my question."

- If he continues with his story, appeal to the judge by saying, "Your Honor, I object. The last part of his answer is nonresponsive, and I ask that it be removed from the record."

Redirect examination

Redirect examination occurs when the prosecuting attorney, if there is one, asks the officer more questions after you complete your cross-examination. The questions asked should only relate to issues that were raised during your cross-examination.

When the prosecutor asks the officer more questions, you are afforded the opportunity to ask the officer more questions. This is referred to as "re-cross examination" and you may ask questions only regarding issues arising out of the prosecutions redirect examination. If you begin to ask irrelevant questions, the prosecution will surely object and the judge will ask you to be seated.

Your Testimony

In most traffic court trials, you will stand up behind the counsel table, look at the judge, and present your case. In some courts, you will be asked to take the witness stand. Wherever you present your case, be prepared. Glance at your notes but do not read them. Here is an example of a rehearsed testimony:

"I was going down Broad Street at 35 miles per hour, in the right lane of a two-lane street.

I glanced in my rearview mirror from time to time. Before I got pulled over, I looked and saw a vehicle about a quarter-mile behind me, gaining speed on me, just as a large truck went by me quickly to my left. I did not know that the car that was gaining speed on me from behind was a police car until the car activated his lights. He was close to my rear fender. At that point, I told my passenger, 'There's an officer flashing his lights. Maybe he's after that other car, so I should let him go.' I pulled over, but he remained behind me."

After concluding your testimony, refer to any diagrams, photos, or other evidence supporting your testimony. Once you have narrated your story and submitted all the evidence you have, the prosecutor, if there is one, will cross-examine you. She will either ask you a few questions or waive the right to cross-examination. The judge will also have the opportunity to ask you a few questions. In some states, the officer may also cross-examine you. However, most states do not allow it.

All of your answers should be provided in a polite, truthful, and concise manner. You are not restricted to "yes" or "no" answers. If you are asked whether you knew you were speeding, reply, "I know I was not speeding because I had just looked at my speedometer." You do not have to merely answer "yes" or "no." Exercise your right.

Witness Testimony

Then, you will have the opportunity to present your eyewitnesses. Depending on how the courtroom is run, you will either have your witness testify in a narrative fashion or ask her questions as to what actually occurred. Here is a sample testimony by a witness:

"Your Honor, on January 25 at about 3:30 p.m., I was sitting in the passenger seat of [your] car. I recollect that just before [you] were pulled over by the officer that we were driving in the right or slow lane. A large truck, among others, was passing us on the left. I then saw colored lights reflected on the windshield and caught a glimpse of the speedometer, which read 35 miles per hour. I am fairly certain I did this before [you] had a chance to slow down."

Practice with your witnesses so you can corroborate your story. Rehearse using both the question and answer-and-narrative method so you are prepared for both. The prosecutor will then get the chance to cross-examine your witness.

Asking Your Witness Questions

It is not easy for a non-legal layperson to ask the right questions. If you feel intimidated by this procedure, say to the judge, "Your Honor, I have not attended law school and I am not familiar with the rules. May I just have my witness tell you what happened?"

If you select — or are asked — to have your witnesses answer questions, especially if you have a prosecutor in the trial, here are some hints that should help you:

- Ask non-leading questions that begin with "what," "who," "where," "when," and "how." Leading questions — which you cannot use when questioning your witness but only during cross-examination — are those questions that provide an answer you are seeking. For example, "What color was the car?" not "The car was red, wasn't it?"

- Avoid extraneous details. For example, it is not necessary to inform the courtroom that you were taking your pet to the vet if you were speeding.

- Avoid questions that presume facts the witness has not testified to. This is another way of saying your questions should aid the witness in explaining what happened in chronological order. For example, do not inquire, "Did you observe a truck passing my car?" This assumes that there was a truck passing your car. This is a fact that the witness has not yet testified to. Simply ask, "Did you see any other vehicles traveling in my direction?" If the witness replies, "Yes, I saw a truck," then you can ask what it was doing.

- Do not ask your witness to retell what was told to her by someone else. That is another example of hearsay. The exception is when the witness testifies about the conversation between you and the ticketing officer, if the officer testified earlier about such conversation.

- Compose a list of the key facts to which your witness will testify. Create a question that will elicit such a fact. Put them in chronological order. Your objective is to build a logical basis for later answers, using the designed answers from earlier questions. For example, you might start with "Where were you on January 25 at 3:30 p.m.?" The assumed answer is "in your car." Then, follow up with "Do you recollect the officer pulling me over?" At that point, ask, "What did you observe before the officer pulled me over?" Your witness can then state how she observed the speedometer was only 35 miles per hour.

Closing statements

The last stage of your traffic court trial is the closing argument or statement. Each side has the opportunity to present its argument after both have introduced their testimonies and evidence and have been permitted to cross-examine witnesses. This is your chance to develop the best arguments you have to be found not guilty. In most states, casting a reasonable doubt to your guilt can do this. In a few states, you must prove your innocence by a preponderance of the evidence — that it is more likely than not that you did not commit the offense. If you have admitted the violation, you must clarify you had a very good reason for technically breaking the law.

If no prosecutor is present, the case normally ends after the officer's testimony and your cross-examination, unless you request to make a final statement. In trials with a prosecuting attorney, she summarizes her case first. She will clarify how the officer's testimony (and perhaps some cross-examination testimony given by you or your witnesses) "proves beyond a reasonable doubt" each element of the offense and disproves any objections you have brought up. Keep calm and poised during the prosecutor's closing statement. It will be a mistake to display rage, bewilderment, or any other emotion, out of respect for the judge. Pay attention and listen carefully to the prosecutor's argument so you can reply to it in your own closing statement.

When a police officer attempts to present a closing statement, object on the grounds that this involves the practice of law. Say something like, "Your Honor, I object. The officer is a witness, not a lawyer or advocate. He is present to provide evidence only, not to be a lawyer by arguing which evidence is more believable, or how this Court should apply law to the facts."

Do not allow the prosecutor to bring in new testimony or evidence during the closing statement. If he does, simply object by saying, "Objection, Your Honor. No evidence was exhibited on that point." When you are your own lawyer in court, you play two roles: witness and advocate. In your role as witness, you have already testified to what you believe occurred. Now, playing the role of attorney, you have the opportunity to review and summarize the main ideas you set forth during the trial and clarify to the judge why the verdict should be not guilty. A closing statement differs from testimony. Behave as if you were a third party, and summarize and comment on the evidence presented during the trial. You are attempting to persuade the judge there is at least a moderate amount of doubt as to your guilt.

Some judges, often when there is no prosecutor present, eliminate the closing argument phase of the trial. Unless you are certain you are going to lose or, conversely, that the judge hinted you will win, you will want to politely assert your right to make a final argument. You can insist by stating, "Your Honor, I believe it is my right to make a final statement. I am organized and concise, but I do want to demonstrate how the evidence proves I am not guilty."

Restrict your closing argument to less than 15 sentences and deliver it in a courteous and convincing manner in order to make a favorable impression. Do not read from notes. Outline your speech ahead of time and rehearse it several days before your court date. If you have the officer's notes, review them carefully for deficiencies and inconsistencies in the conclusions he arrives at. You may have to edit your speech somewhat after hearing the officer's testimony, but this should not be difficult if you plan what you are going to say. Finish your closing argument with, "And for these reasons, Your Honor, there is a reasonable doubt as to whether I committed the offense, and I therefore ask that you find me not guilty."

Below are three things to avoid in your closing argument:

1. Do not bring up new ideas you or other witnesses have not already testified to. You must only refer to facts presented at the trial.

2. Do not be personal. Do not insult the officer by claiming he discriminated against you. You may, though, point out flaws in his testimony or your cross-examination of him if he neglected to give convincing or complete answers to your questions.

3. Do not be belligerent by threatening not to heed to the court's decision regarding your case or to challenge their authority to ticket you in the first place.

Your closing statement, which you deliver after the prosecution side makes theirs, should highlight that at least one of the aspects of the offense has not been proven beyond a reasonable doubt. On the other hand, you can argue you have presented some other defense.

Start your closing argument by saying to the judge, "Your Honor, I would like to summarize how the evidence points to my not being guilty." Then, clarify how:

- The officer's testimony failed to prove one or more aspects of the citation — and which ones

- Your testimony, and that of your witnesses, has demonstrated you did not transgress one or more elements despite the officer's testimony to the contrary

- Your testimony establishes a legally sufficient reason why you had a right to violate the statute, such as your reaction to a dire emergency

The following is an example of a closing argument:

"Your Honor, let me briefly recap the evidence to show you I am not guilty. First, the officer never really set forth that I violated [code section you are charged with] when he depended heavily on his notes and could not clearly recall what actually occurred. When I cross-examined him, he honestly admitted:

- That he had not calibrated the radar unit with a tuning fork at the start and end of his work day, as is suggested in the radar unit's instruction manual.

- That he was more than 180 feet away from my vehicle when he turned on the radar unit."

"By contrast, both my witness and I testified I was in the right or slow lane, and that we were surrounded by traffic in both directions, including a large truck passing ahead of me in the lane to my left. Moreover, the officer admitted in his testimony it took him at least three seconds to aim the radar unit at my vehicle, signifying that my car was about 180 feet in front of his, and receding, when he turned it on. He also admitted that at that distance, the radar beam was at least 30 feet wide, which is the same width as two lanes. Finally, he also reluctantly admitted that his radar unit is more sensitive to a larger target, such as a large truck, and that it is entirely plausible to obtain an erroneous reading in a case like this."

"Finally, my witness and I testified I was driving approximately 35 miles per hour based on glancing at my speedometer, which I proved was accurate. To summarize, I believe in this case there certainly is reasonable doubt as to whether the officer correctly observed my car's speed, and I therefore respectfully ask that you find me not guilty."

Since the burden of proving you guilty lies with the prosecutor, he gets two opportunities to argue his case. In the second one, the prosecution's rebuttal statement, the prosecution responds to what you covered in your closing argument. Often, the prosecutor waives the right to make a rebuttal statement. An officer almost never will make a rebuttal statement.

The verdict

After all the evidence has been submitted and the closing statements have been made, the judge must declare his verdict or take the case "under advisement" or "under submission." This signifies the judge wants to contemplate it.

When the judge takes the case under advisement, it means you will be notified of the verdict by mail. However, if you are contemplating appealing the case should you lose, it is wise to telephone or visit the court once a week to determine whether the verdict has been filed. The reason for this is because in most areas your appeal to a higher court must be filed between five and 30 days from the time the judge files the verdict with the court clerk, and some court clerks do not mail the paperwork in a timely manner. This can result in not enough time to appeal. When the judge finds you not guilty, you do not need to pay a fine and any and all bail monies are returned to you.

The sentence

In most states, for routine citations, judges give the amount of your fine right after announcing a guilty verdict. If you put together a decent defense but did not persuade the judge of your innocence, the judge may lower or even waive the fine. In a few states, if you are found guilty and fined, the judge may listen to a plea (or read a letter) from you requesting a reduction or suspension of fine based on your good driving record or any other persuasive reason. Or, the judge may agree to a payment schedule if you cannot pay the fine in one lump sum. Talk to the clerk regarding a fine reduction.

Appealing

The chances of overturning your verdict by appealing for a new trial are small if you did not persuade the judge of your innocence in the first trial. Despite the fact every state provides a person the right to appeal, the procedure is extremely tedious involving a great deal of time and expense. To summarize, before you appeal, think about whether it is worth the time and effort.

In broad terms, there are two types of appeals. One type only permits an appeal on the record — that means an appellate court will overturn the trial court only if the trial court committed a legal mistake. The second type of appeal — called "trial de novo" — permits you a second trial. Some states allow one type, others allow the other type, but few allow both. You have a better opportunity to win when you get a new trial.

In states where new trials are permitted, you will have to show up in court before a judge and plead your case again. There are at least three reasons to think about this approach:

- If the judge at your first trial was prejudiced against traffic court defendants. In this case, check with the court clerk to determine whether judges are randomly chosen or if a different court would handle your appeal. You might get a less punitive judge in your appeal.

- If you did a poor job presenting your case the first time around. If you were nervous, unprepared, and intimidated by a prosecutor or a judge, you probably learned from the experience and could do a better job second time around.

- In approximately 12 states, a "de novo" trial is the first chance you have to appeal to a jury. It can be said that jurors are more congenial to defendants than judges are. As a result, you might get a better chance at a not guilty verdict if you appeal with a jury trial. Note: There might be fees for the second trial. Call the clerk's office.

What about the type of appeal made to an appellate court that only grants a new trial if there is a legal error? Here, your chances of a reversal in decision are slim to none. The appellate court will almost always conclude that the judge conducted the trial justly and applied the law correctly. It ignores trivial procedural glitches, for example, the judge let the officer read his notes, which you might have objected to. Consult a lawyer if you wish to take your case to the appellate court, as it is a time-consuming and complicated procedure.

CHAPTER 15

Jury Trial

Many defense lawyers will say a jury trial is more advantageous for a defendant. It is true, but you must prepare more carefully as it is a more complicated procedure. You will need to pick a jury — and unlike bench trials where you normally face only the arresting officer, an experienced prosecutor will be assigned who knows how to present evidence. Therefore, even in states that permit jury trials, many defendants select a trial with a judge only.

On the other hand, there are good reasons to ask for a jury trial. The most important one is if you make a persuasive presentation, a jury will more than likely side with you. That is because many people feel they have been victimized by the traffic system and will be more sympathetic to your case. If you face serious repercussions from a guilty verdict, such as losing your license or a huge increase in your insurance premiums, consider asking for a jury trial.

The format of a jury trial is just like a formal bench trial. The one difference is that you must select a jury. *Bench trials were discussed in Chapter 14.*

Jury Selection

Attorneys agree that choosing members of a jury is the most important phase of the trial. As the defendant, you want to send certain people away, such as those who are closed-minded or sympathetic to police officers. This is because they will not usually vote for acquittal no matter how strong a case you set forth. You do want jurors who are open-minded, willing to be attentive to both sides, and at least a little skeptical of police and a prosecutor's powers. Remember, even though you are standing up for your rights, it is usually a mistake to treat the case like a murder trial and contest every technical procedural move. Keep things polite and professional in the courtroom.

Jury selection normally starts as soon as the judge calls your case and after the resolution of any preliminary motions. Potential jurors will gather in a "jury assembly room" where you have no contact with them. In some courtrooms, they sit in the hallways or the courtroom. If you run into a potential juror, do not discuss your case with him or her because this is considered tampering with the jury. Do not speak with jurors at all until your trial is over and your verdict has been handed out.

During the questioning stage, determine whether any juror is biased or will view you negatively. This is called "voir dire," or "to speak the truth." In many states, the judge will ask the questions herself. She will aim the questions at the entire panel of jurors, not individual ones. These questions will often be general and ask their occupation, spouse's occupation, previous encounters with the criminal justice system, and relationships with police and attorneys. For example, a judge may ask:

- "Are any of you acquainted with the defendant, the witness, or the officer?"

- "Are any of you employed with the police, the district attorney's office, or any other law enforcement agency?"

- "Are any of you related to or have close friends who work in law enforcement or in a district attorney's office?"

- "Is there any reason any of you potential jurors cannot render an impartial and unbiased decision?"

If a potential juror admits to having a prejudice that could bias her in the case, the judge will excuse that juror "for cause" without further words from you. After the judge is finished questioning the jurors, you will be allowed to further question them in an attempt to screen out jurors who may be prejudiced against you. When the judge excuses a juror, a new juror replaces him or her. Then, the judge may ask additional questions of these new jurors or, if they have been in the courtroom, ask if they heard the questions and request a response to them.

After the judge has completed questioning, indicate that you accept the jury with no further questioning. There can be times when you would like to question the jurors further, but you should refrain.

"Voir dire" questions

If you are given the opportunity to ask questions of the potential jurors, do not ask the same questions that the judge and prosecutor asked. Pursue any unsatisfactory answers by requesting more detail. When you are requested to ask questions aimed at the panel of jurors, ask these:

- "Do any of you object to being jurors for a traffic court case? If you do, please raise your hand."

- "Do any of you object that I am representing myself instead of using an attorney?"

- "Do any of you have an issue with believing one is innocent until proven guilty beyond a reasonable doubt based on evidence?"

- "Have any of you ever worked as a police officer or security guard in the past?"

- "Do any of you have friends or relatives who have worked as police officer, security guards, or for the district attorney's office?"

- "Is there anyone who would believe a police officer's testimony over my testimony merely because he or she is a police officer?" Exercise your challenge if someone answers in the affirmative for this question.

- "Do any one of you think police officers rarely make mistakes in their observations?"

- "Do any one of you think a police officer always tells the truth unconditionally?"

- "Have any one of you ever been a juror before where the defendant was charged with the offense I am charged with?" If someone answers "yes," ask "Did that jury reach a verdict?" If "yes" you should assume the verdict was "guilty" and exercise your challenge.

- "Have any of you ever been in a car accident that you thought was caused by someone violating the law?" If "yes," ask about the details of the accident and how he thinks the other person broke the law. If it was a recent accident, and the other person broke the same law you are on trial for, exercise your challenge.

- "Are there any one of you who do not drive or drive less than 5,000 miles each year?" A person who takes mass transit or does not drive often may not be as sympathetic as a traveling salesman who drives 20,000 miles a year.

- "Have any of you have never received a ticket?" You probably want to disqualify anyone who has never received a ticket because he or she probably will not be sympathetic to you.

If a juror says something that suggests he will not be fair, ask follow-up questions. For example, you could say, "Mr. Smith, I saw that you nodded slightly when I asked you if you had any friends or relatives in the police department. Was that a yes?" You might ask further questions to reveal a possible bias toward you and a pro-police leaning. If you wish to excuse that person, use one of your preemptory challenges or, if he is obviously prejudiced, ask the judge to excuse the juror for cause.

Challenging a juror

Two reasons you may wish to remove a person from the jury are:

1. The person exhibits a clear bias against you.

2. You get a bad feeling about a juror for some unknown reason.

There are two ways in which to remove a juror you do not want.

Challenges for cause

When a prospective juror clearly shows that he is biased, the judge may disqualify him before you get the chance to question him. However, if this does not happen, you must wait until you are provided a chance to make a challenge and ask the judge to disqualify that person for cause. Simply say to the judge, "Your

Honor, I respectfully challenge potential juror Jones for cause because of his declaration that he would find it difficult to be fair in light of his statement that his mother was hurt by someone who was speeding."

The judge will agree to dismiss a juror for cause for the following reasons:

- The potential juror, or his close friend or relation, was hurt by someone who committed the same type of violation you are on trial for, and the juror confesses he would have difficulty being objective.

- The potential juror admits he would believe the testimony of a police officer instead of your testimony simply because the witness was a police officer.

- The potential juror is a close friend of or related to the officer or any other prosecution witness, or of the prosecuting attorney.

- The potential juror heard about your case before being summoned to court as a juror and has indicated some opinion about your guilt.

When the judge disagrees with you and refuses to disqualify the juror, you still have another option to get him off the panel.

Peremptory (automatic) challenges

In most states, you are entitled to excuse a specific number of potential jurors for any reason, or for no particular reason at all. The amount of "peremptory" challenges you are permitted varies from state to state depending on the violation you are charged with and how large the jury is. With a 12-person jury, it would be common for you and the prosecutor to each have from three to ten peremptory challenges. When the jury is a six-member jury, you might be permitted only two to five challenges. Since this is an area that differs from state to state, consult the clerk court in your state.

When challenging a juror, it is advisable to trust your instincts. If you get what is known as "bad vibes" from someone, even without reason, remove him or her from the jury. In addition to trusting your instincts, when the judge does not disqualify them himself, it is advisable to consider instituting peremptory challenges for the following types of people:

- Current and former police officers and security guards, their significant others, and children.

- Anyone who has ever been employed in a prosecutor's office, including lawyers, paralegals, and support staff.

- Relations or close friends of the above-mentioned professions.

- Anyone who has ever been involved in an accident or had a relation involved in an accident caused by someone who was charged with the same violation as you.

- People who do not drive or have never received a ticket.

- People who exhibit non-verbal gestures that indicate they are annoyed at having been called for jury duty.

- People who give you "bad vibes" for any reason.

- People whose dress and lifestyle differ dramatically from yours. Please note, though, the Constitution prevents you from striking someone solely because of his or her race or gender.

After the jury is chosen, the jurors are "sworn in" by the judge or clerk. Then, the trial begins in much the same manner as a trial before a judge.

Opening Statements

Although some opening statements are not given during a traffic ticket court trial before a judge, you should not forego the opportunity to present your opening statement before jurors. It is very important to make a first impression on jurors and get them on your side from the beginning. Keep in mind you have the option to present your opening statement after the prosecutor gives his or waives it as the case may be. You can also save your opening statement until you cross-examine the officer before you give your testimony. It is best, though, to give it as soon as possible before the jury because they often make up their minds early on in the trial — sometimes dependent upon your opening statement. If you put off your opening statement until later in the trial, jurors who have only heard the prosecution may have already made up their minds as to your guilt or innocence before you have even presented your case.

Stand up behind the counsel table and face the jury when presenting your opening statement. Do not walk or pace around the courtroom. Stand up straight, look jurors right in the eyes and tell them in a concise manner the evidence you will provide to prove your innocence. You may glance at notes, but if you have rehearsed your opening statement with friends or relatives at home, it should not be necessary to read them. Finally, opening statements are to tell the jury what the facts of the case will show. This is not the time to make legal arguments beyond the simple statement that after all the evidence they will have no choice but to find you not guilty.

Your presentation to the jury has more influence than it would have on a judge. Be straightforward. Keep in mind how you present yourself during the opening statement will have a huge bearing on the jury — more so than on a judge. Do not be sarcastic or insulting, even if the arresting officer mistreated you. Assume instead that the officer made an honest mistake you now want to correct — with the help of a jury.

The Prosecution's Testimony

In jury trials, the officer will always testify and answer the prosecutor's questions. You are entitled to object to improper questions, but in a jury trial you should reserve your objections for critical issues. Jurors normally resent the side that tries to conceal information from them and may rule against the side that objects the most. Moreover, trying to keep evidence from a jury may go against you. Even when the judge backs up your objection, jurors are likely to surmise what was left out and assign more importance to it than if you did not object and allowed the evidence. Despite taking these precautions, if the prosecutor crosses the line in your estimation, you will still probably want to object.

Your Cross-Examination

Be polite and firm when you cross-examine the prosecution's witnesses. When the officer rambles on and tells more than you think is relevant, interrupt and direct her to, "Please answer the question. You've already had a chance to tell your story. Please do not try to persuade the jury further."

Your Testimony

- Make your opening statement at the start of the trial. If you have not made it at the beginning of the trial, be certain to make it before your testimony. Then, your testimony in a jury trial should proceed like in a bench trial.

- Look at the jurors and make eye contact. You want them to see you as an honest, law-abiding citizen who has been wrongly accused.

- Observe jurors for non-verbal signs and reactions during your testimony to determine if you are getting your point across or just confusing them.

- Adapt your conduct to jurors' reactions.

- When your testimony is finished, and after the prosecutor has cross-examined you, present your witnesses.

- Your witnesses can testify in a narrative fashion or in response to guiding questions from you. If the judge suggests you question the witnesses, you may say you are unfamiliar with the manner in which such questions should be asked, and would like your witness to proceed in a narrative fashion. If the judge declines your request, be prepared to ask your witness questions.

Judges generally remain poker-faced even while listening to the most obvious nonsense. On the other hand, jurors are not trained this way nor do they wish to remain impartial. Therefore, be on the lookout for nonverbal signals that might suggest confusion or skepticism on the part of one or more jurors regarding your testimony, and adapt your behavior accordingly.

After you have completed your testimony, the prosecutor has the opportunity to cross-examine you. Be attentive to each question.

If you do not fully comprehend the question, ask the prosecutor to explain it. If you comprehend the question but do not know how to respond, admit it while keeping in mind that you are entitled to explain your answer even when your answer is, "I don't know." Conversely, do not avoid responding to clear questions — otherwise the jury will think you are trying to hide something.

To repeat, always be courteous. It is unwise to be rude or aggressive to the prosecutor because in a close case, this can be the deciding factor against you. How you answer the cross-examination by the prosecutor should be the same as in a bench trial except in a jury trial you should look at the jurors and try to make eye contact and read their reactions.

Closing Arguments

After all the evidence is presented and testimonies heard, both you and the prosecutor will have the chance to give closing arguments. Delivering a closing statement to a jury is far more vital than presenting one to a judge in a non-jury trial. Judges take pride in delivering a verdict based on evidence and not the closing statements. Jurors are far less decisive as to the legal ramifications of your evidence and are far more inclined to listen to why you think you are not guilty.

Remain calm and expressionless during the prosecution's closing argument. Do not express rage, frustration, indignation, shock, or any other emotion no matter how much the prosecution twists the truth. Just listen carefully and take notes so you can modify your closing argument accordingly.

Your closing argument should accomplish two things. First, you want to clarify clearly how the evidence that was presented at the trial is not enough to determine your guilt beyond a reasonable doubt or, in fact, actually disproves it. Second, you should counter damaging statements made by the prosecutor in her arguments. For example, if the prosecutor states you entered an intersection when the signal was already red, you will wish to explain the fact that the officer had a bad viewing angle and was preoccupied at the time.

It is also vital to point out to the jurors, at both the start and end of your closing argument, that each element of the offense must be established "beyond a reasonable doubt." Although legally this falls somewhere between "great" doubt and "insignificant" doubt, it is correct to declare that a "reasonable" juror who has any doubt at all about your guilt, should find you innocent. Since most people think of themselves as reasonable, it is your hope that any juror who has any doubt will cast a vote of not guilty. In states that permit jury trials for traffic violations, most still require unanimous votes in order to reach a verdict. In these states, even one dissenting vote results in a "hung" jury with no conviction.

The following is an example of a closing argument:

"Ladies and gentlemen of the jury, because I am sure I am innocent of the offense(s) charged, I am contesting them here. Attorneys are costly, and so I am defending myself. Although I do not have any training in the legal profession, I have proven my case as best as I know how to demonstrate to you why I am not guilty. There is one thing I am certain about regarding the American legal system — the prosecution must prove every defendant, myself included, guilty of each facet of an offense beyond a reasonable doubt. Now, I want to clarify exactly why the prosecution has not successfully accomplished that in my case."

Next, clarify the facets of the offense and how, in regards to the evidence presented, and based on your testimony, evidence, and any witnesses, doubt as to your guilt still exists.

"You have been presented with my evidence, and the testimony of my witnesses. You have also heard from the police officer. These are conflicting accounts of what occurred. Please do not think the officer's powers of observations are foolproof just because he is a police officer. And please do not believe uncritically what the prosecutor said when she repeated the officer's accounts of events. Neither the prosecutor nor the police officer disproved any of the evidence my witnesses nor I set forth. Keep in mind, if the law demanded you to believe law enforcement personnel are perfect, we would not have any trials at all. So, again, please consider my version of the story — I have been as honest as I can be. When I am done speaking, the prosecutor is permitted another opportunity to undermine my argument. She may tell you that I have a lot to gain by being not guilty and therefore, the officer's account is more plausible than mine. I harbor no ill feelings toward the officer, and I realize part of the reason she patrols the roads is to protect us from hazardous drivers. However, she is not perfect and in this instance she was erroneous. Finally, you will recall that in the beginning of this case, you each swore that you would protect my rights and honor my Constitutional guarantee that I am not guilty until and unless the prosecution proves each element of the offense I am charged with beyond a reasonable doubt. Indeed, the prosecution has failed to do this in my case. In returning to the jury room to deliberate, I respectfully request to do your duty in this regard and to enter a verdict of not guilty. Thank you."

This speech might seem long-winded, but when you speak, it is short. Tailor it to your particular case, and practice it before going to trial.

The prosecutor gets her second opportunity to rebut your case after the closing argument. Sometimes, the prosecutor will waive this opportunity. Other times, she will make a brief statement.

Jury Instructions

After you have presented your evidence, you have the chance to submit proposed "jury instructions" to be read to the jury by the judges. Since most judges are required and do a good job at this for normal cases, you should leave this task to the judge. If the judge is hostile, you will want to do it yourself.

A law library will include books judges most often utilize in your state. Skim through these books to traffic offenses. A judge must provide a jury instruction at your request if evidence supports it. For example, if your testimony said you had to speed to the hospital with your wife, who was actually giving birth, the judge is required to read the jury instruction on the "necessity defense."

The standard instructions, which the judge provides, include clarifying to jurors how they are to comprehend the duties of the judge and jury, and how they are supposed to consider various types of evidence and how to ascertain the trustworthiness of witnesses. Finally, the judge will clarify the presumption of innocence. He or she will say: "A defendant in a criminal action is presumed to be innocent until the contrary is proved, and in case of a reasonable doubt as to whether his guilt is proven, he is entitled to a verdict of not guilty. This presumption places on the State the burden of proving him guilty beyond a reasonable doubt." He or she will then go on to define reasonable doubt. "It is not a mere possible doubt, because everything relating to human affairs, and depending on moral evidence, is suspect to doubt. It is the state of the case that after the entire comparison and consideration of the evidence, leaves the minds of the jurors in that condition, such that they cannot say they feel an abiding conviction, to a certainty, of the truth of the charge."

The judge will finally instruct the jury from the standard instructions, in addition to any instructions the judge accepted from you or the prosecutor. The bailiff will then lead the jury into the jury room to deliberate a verdict. When they return, they will announce a verdict. If you are guilty, the judge will sentence you at a later date.

Appeals from a Jury Verdict

When you receive a guilty verdict from a jury trial, your chances of successfully appealing are very slim because in the vast majority of states, you are not entitled to a new ("de novo") trial.

Instead, the appellate court will simply examine whether the trial court judge followed the law (called an appeal "on the record" or "on the law"). Even then, the error has to be egregious to catch the attention of the appeals court and overturn your sentence. The appeals process is complicated, expensive, and rarely makes sense for traffic cases.

CONCLUSION

Traffic tickets can be an expensive and troublesome problem. Most people accept them as a part of life and grudgingly pay them. Stand-up comics make jokes about them, but even they are vulnerable and find them burdensome. Traffic court judges find them trivial, jurors resent having to preside over a traffic court trial, but the fact remains: When you receive a traffic ticket, you must deal with it.

This book's main objective is to provide a solution when you receive a ticket. This book has boldly suggested taking it to the source and fighting it. Many people never consider doing this, and others have successfully fought and won. Instead of assuming a victim's mentality, you should fight the ticket.

This book has covered all facets of traffic court tickets to strengthen your case. The law is presented in terms of the two types of traffic violations as well as the types of speeding violations. You now know the ramifications of whether you should fight your ticket or pay it, even when you know you are in the right.

You have received an overview on how police measure your speed from a technical standpoint — so should you take your case to court, you know if you have a case.

You will need a lawyer for more serious offenses such as a DUI. However, you can handle most other traffic tickets alone. There is extensive coverage of questions for cross-examination, as well as detailed summaries of courtroom procedure. Now it is time to get the courage to organize and prepare your case for your day in court. You can do it by studying this book. Stand up for your rights.

APPENDIX

Glossary

Affidavit — A statement of an individual sworn to under penalty of perjury.

Appeal — The process of asking a higher court to review the judgment of a lower court for errors.

Arraignment — A preliminary hearing where a person charged with an offense enters a plea to the charge of either guilty, not guilty, or no contest (nolo contendere).

Bench Trial — Trial in front of a judge, without a jury operating as the finder of fact.

Bench Warrant — A warrant issued by a judge to a witness or party to a case for failure to appear in court as directed by either a summons or subpoena.

Challenge for Cause — Challenging the eligibility of a potential juror to serve on a jury because a perceived bias that juror holds.

Closing Statement — Statement delivered by the parties after all the evidence has been presented. Closing statements serve to summarize the evidence and argue where the evidence points to judgment in the arguing party's favor.

Continuance — The postponement of a hearing. To receive a continuance you must either file a motion to continue with the court, or move the court orally for a continuance at a hearing.

Court Clerk — The administrative agent of the court who handles the filings and scheduling of hearings.

Cross Examination — Examination of a witness by the party who did not call the witness to testify.

De Novo Trial — A new trial. Nothing presented at a previous trial matters for purposes of the new trial.

Direct Examination — Examination of a witness by the party who called that witness to testify.

Discovery — The process whereby a party to an action obtains non-privileged, relevant information from either another party or a third party. Discovery can take the form of interrogatories, depositions, or admissions, among other forms.

Felony — Serious crimes that carry substantial periods of jail time and large fines.

Hearsay — An out-of-court statement offered for the truth of the matter asserted. Persons testifying in court must have direct knowledge of that to which they are testifying; absent limited exceptions, they cannot testify as to matters related to them by a third party.

Misdemeanor — Lower level of crime, usually carrying short periods of jail time and small fines.

Motion — A document submitted to the court asking the judge to act in some way (for example: motion to continue, motion to quash subpoena, motion to vacate judgment).

Opening Statement — Statement delivered by parties at the beginning of a trial. Presented prior to a party putting on evidence.

Per Se — "As a matter of law."

Peremptory Challenges — Challenges by a party to a potential juror sitting on a jury. Exercised during the jury selection process and limited by law to a specific number.

Pro Se — The legal term for when a party represents him or herself in court.

Rebuttal — A second closing statement given by the prosecution after the defendant has presented his closing statements. Rebuttals are limited to issues brought up in the opposition's closing statement.

Re-cross examination — Examination of the witness by the party who did not call the witness. Occurs after re-direct examination and is limited in scope to the issues raised by the opposing party during their re-direct examination.

Re-direct Examination — Examination of the witness by the party who called the witness to testify. Occurs after cross-examination and is limited to the scope of issues raised by the opposing party during their cross examination.

Retainer — Fee paid to an attorney for agreeing to take on a case, or a fee paid to an attorney before the need arises to ensure the attorney is available to take a case should the need arise. Retainers are usually applied as a down payment toward legal costs.

Sentence — The penalty handed down by the court upon disposition of a case.

Statute — Laws enacted by a legislative body (for example: state legislature, federal legislature) and codified in the codes of that jurisdiction.

Subpoena — Legal process demanding that a third-party appear. You can issue a subpoena to appear for a deposition, a trial, or to bring physical evidence (a subpoena duces tecum).

Under Advisement — When a judge decides to consider the evidence outside of the courtroom prior to making a decision. Often, this decision will be issued in a writing by the court.

Voir Dire — The process of selecting a jury.

BIBLIOGRAPHY

D.W. Brown, *Beat Your Ticket — Go to Court & WIN*. Nolo Press, Berkeley, CA (2007)

Alex Carroll, *Beat the Cops — The Guide to Fighting Your Traffic Ticket and Winning*. AceCo Publishers, Santa Barbara, CA (2005)

Robert Schachner, *How and When To Be Your Own Lawyer*. Perigee Publishers, New York, NY (2000)

AUTHOR BIOGRAPHY

An ex-New Yorker who relocated to Southern California, Janet Traken is a freelance writer who has written six books and has published in national publications, such as *Hits Magazine, Today's Caregiver,* and *The Advocate.* She was a senior editor at a legal, business, and financial self-help publisher. Her novel, *How to Forget Your Life,* can be read at **www.publicbookshelf.com**.

INDEX

T

U

V

Y